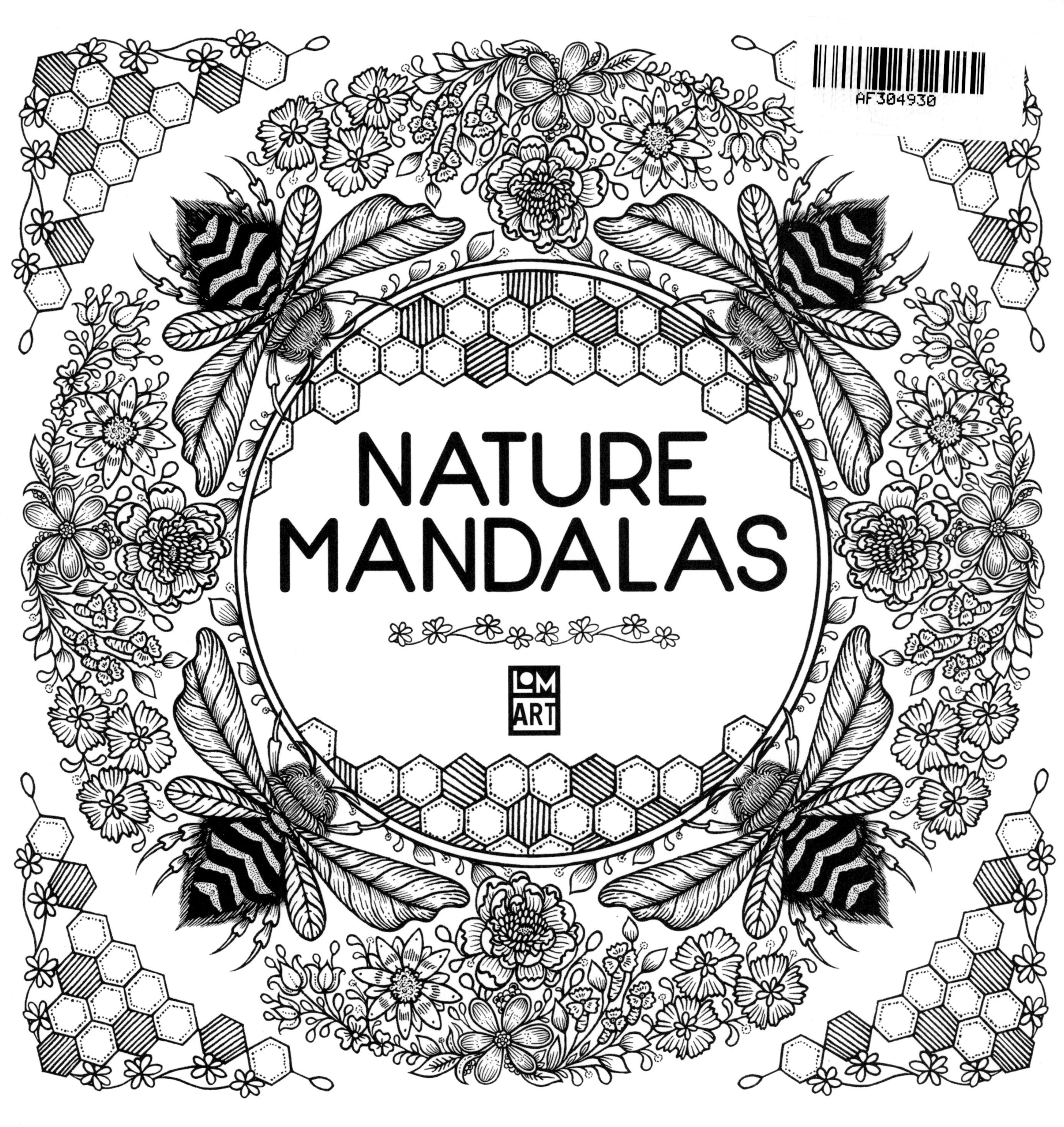

NATURE
MANDALAS
LOM ART

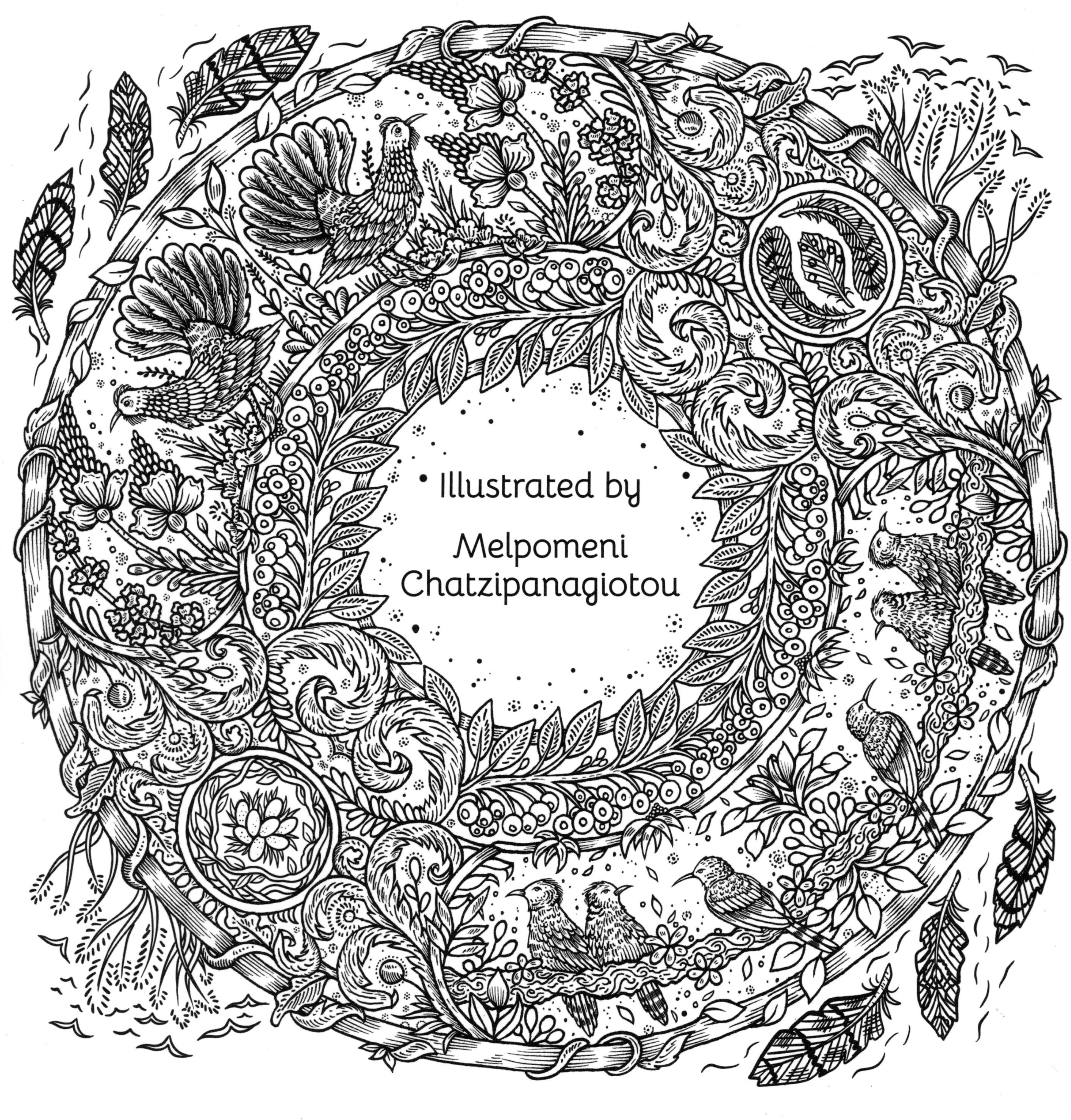

Illustrated by

Melpomeni
Chatzipanagiotou

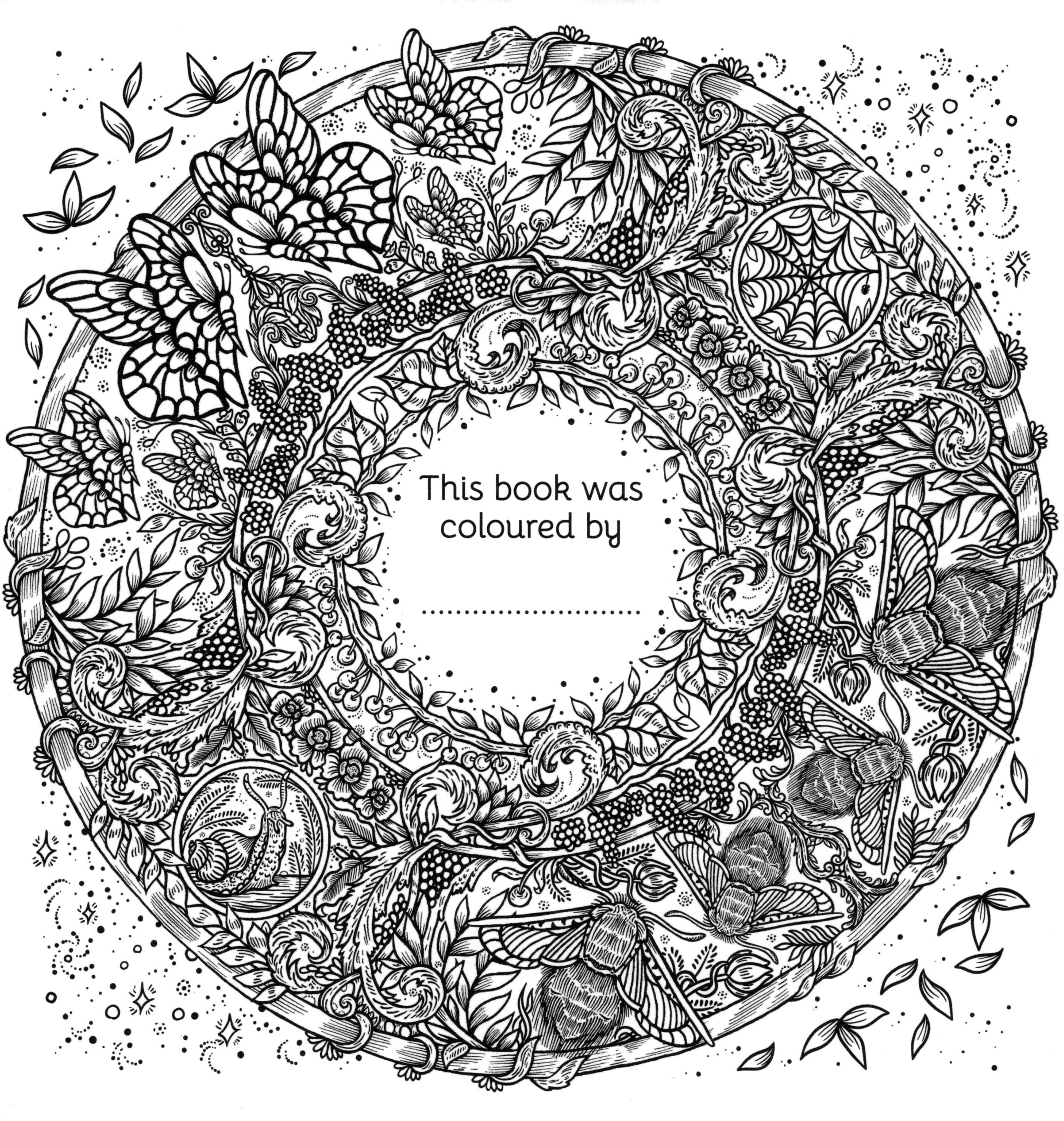
This book was
coloured by

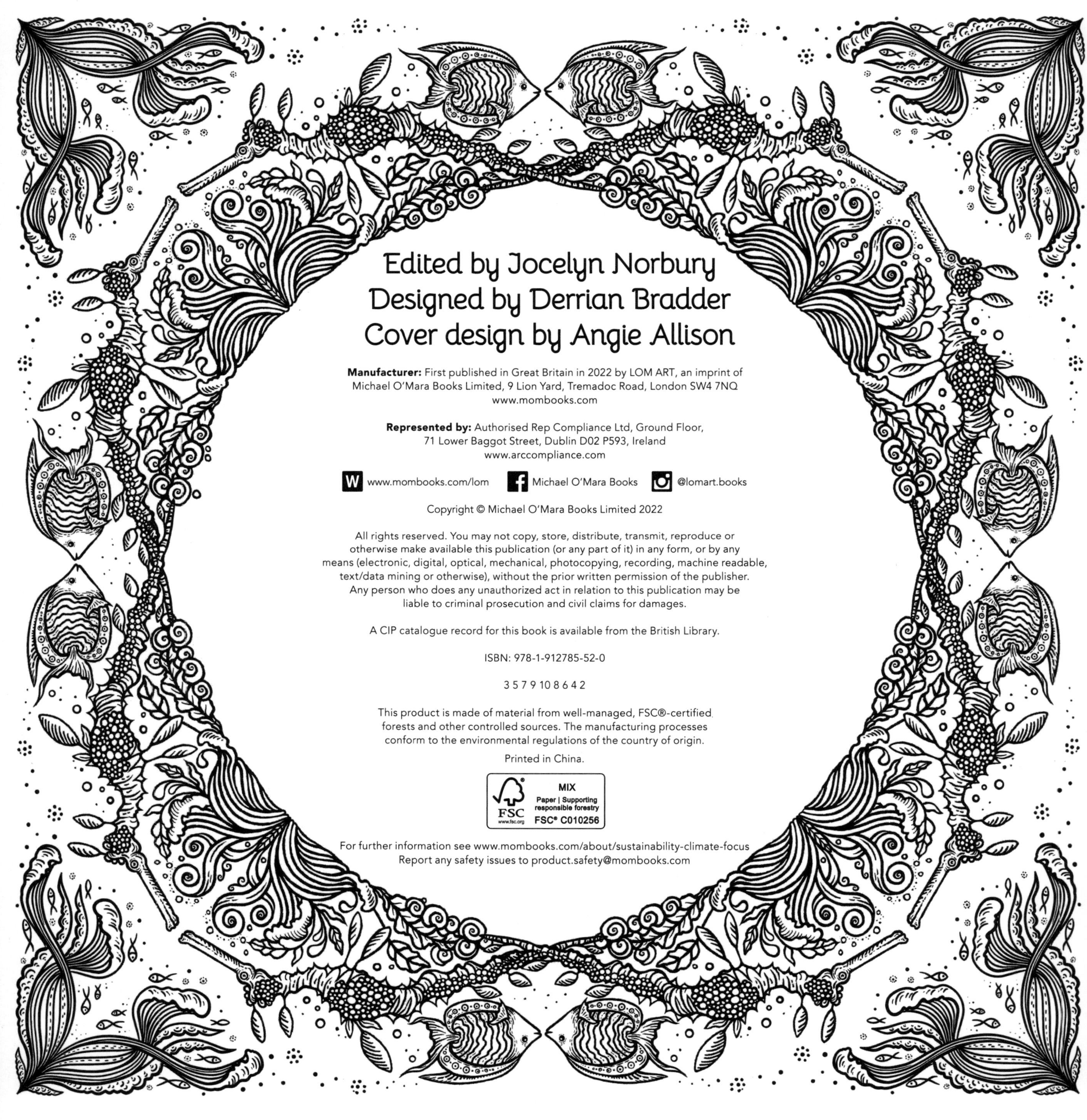

Edited by Jocelyn Norbury
Designed by Derrian Bradder
Cover design by Angie Allison

Manufacturer: First published in Great Britain in 2022 by LOM ART, an imprint of
Michael O'Mara Books Limited, 9 Lion Yard, Tremadoc Road, London SW4 7NQ
www.mombooks.com

Represented by: Authorised Rep Compliance Ltd, Ground Floor,
71 Lower Baggot Street, Dublin D02 P593, Ireland
www.arccompliance.com

W www.mombooks.com/lom   f Michael O'Mara Books   @lomart.books

A CIP catalogue record for this book is available from the British Library.

ISBN: 978-1-912785-52-0

3 5 7 9 10 8 6 4 2

This product is made of material from well-managed, FSC®-certified
forests and other controlled sources. The manufacturing processes
conform to the environmental regulations of the country of origin.

Printed in China.

MIX
Paper | Supporting
responsible forestry
FSC® C010256

For further information see www.mombooks.com/about/sustainability-climate-focus
Report any safety issues to product.safety@mombooks.com

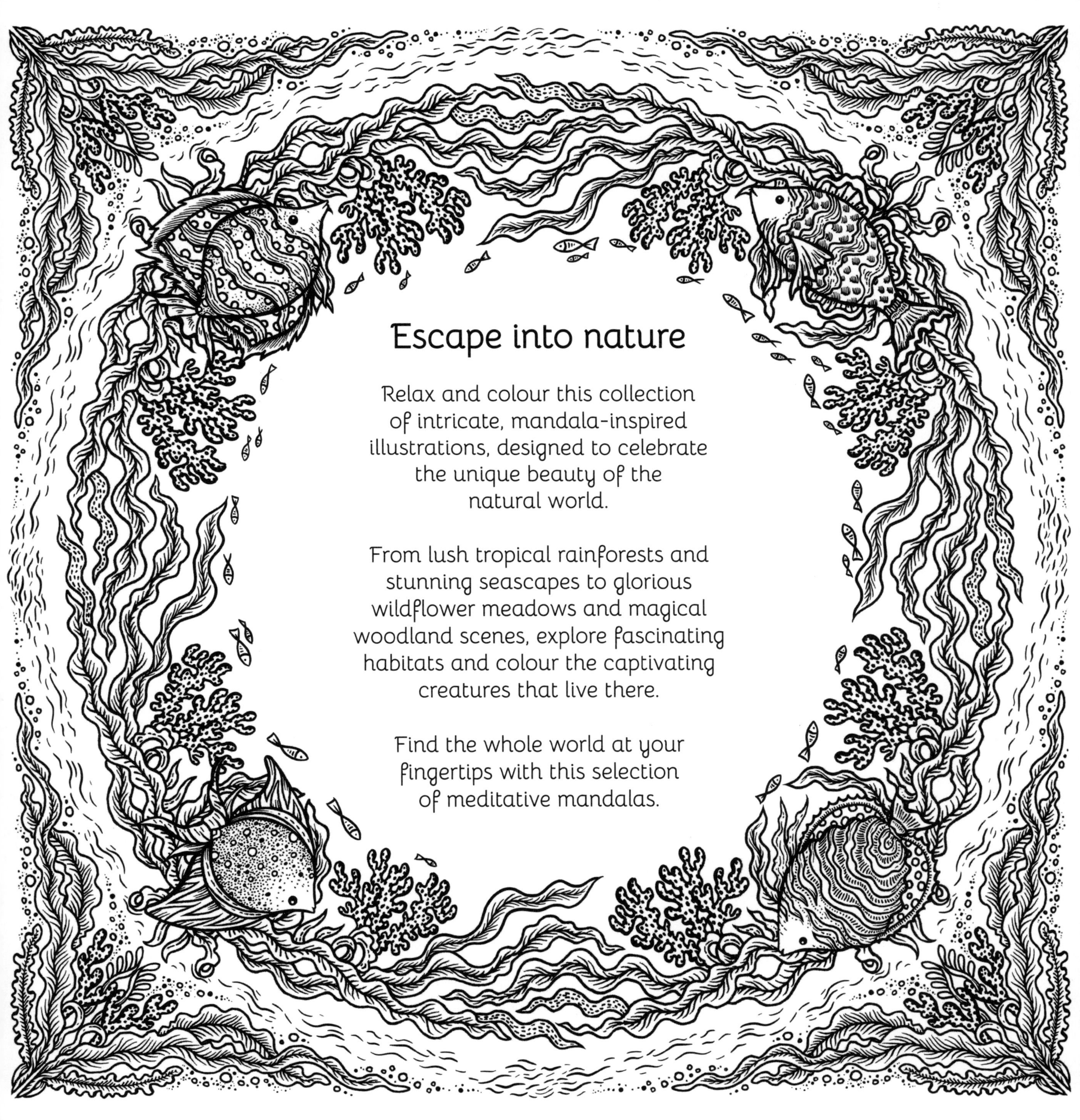

Escape into nature

Relax and colour this collection
of intricate, mandala-inspired
illustrations, designed to celebrate
the unique beauty of the
natural world.

From lush tropical rainforests and
stunning seascapes to glorious
wildflower meadows and magical
woodland scenes, explore fascinating
habitats and colour the captivating
creatures that live there.

Find the whole world at your
fingertips with this selection
of meditative mandalas.

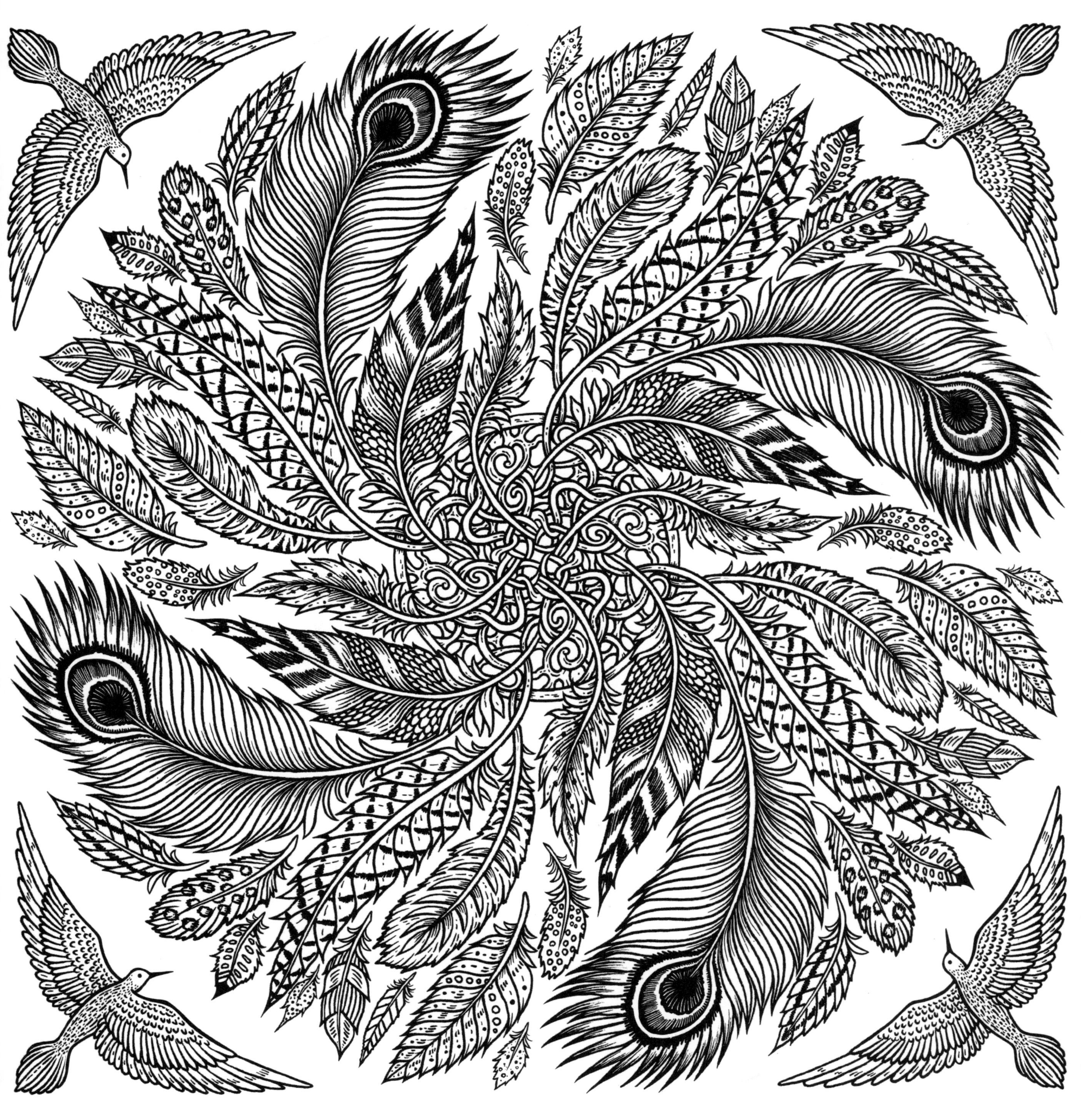

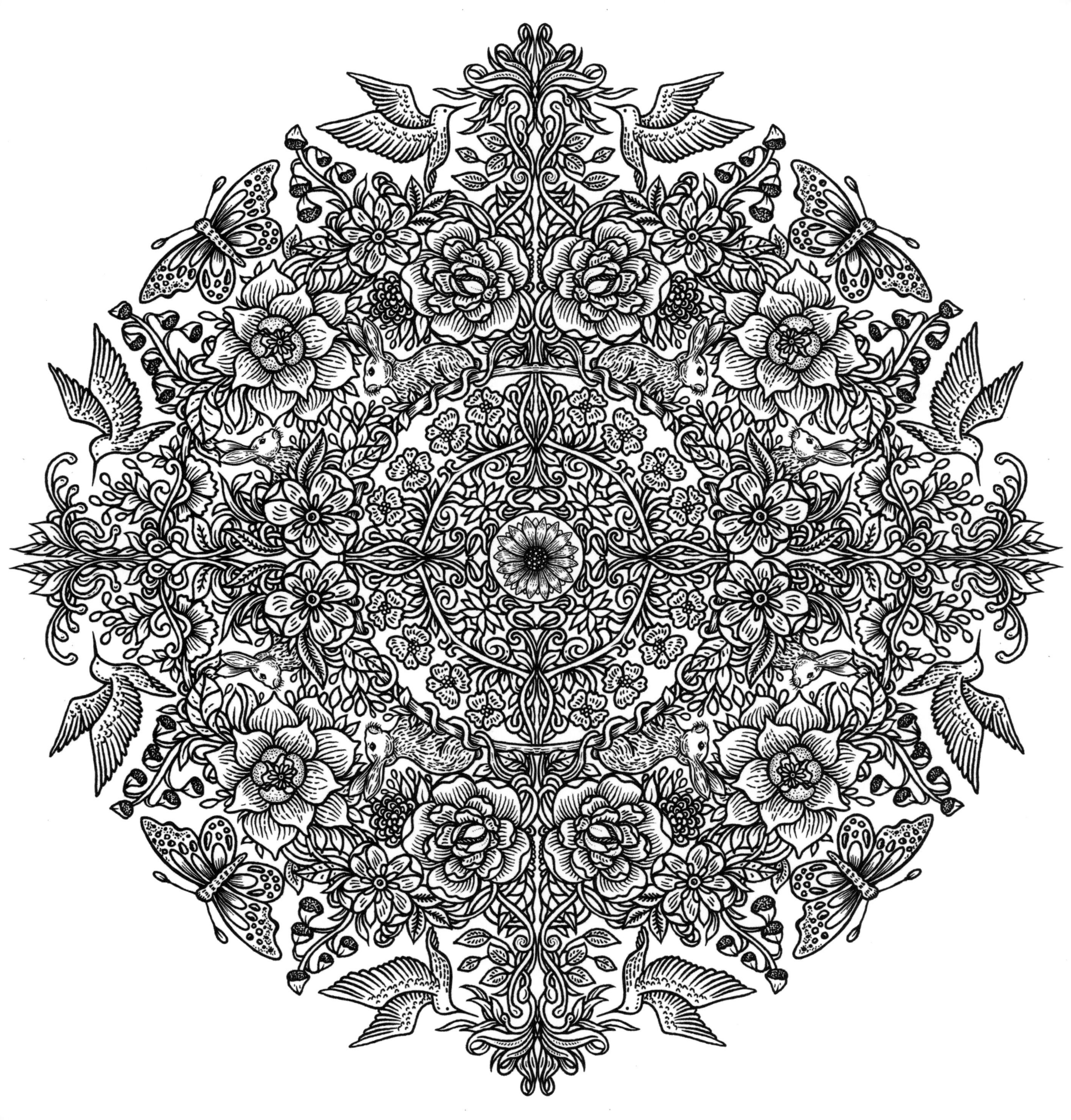

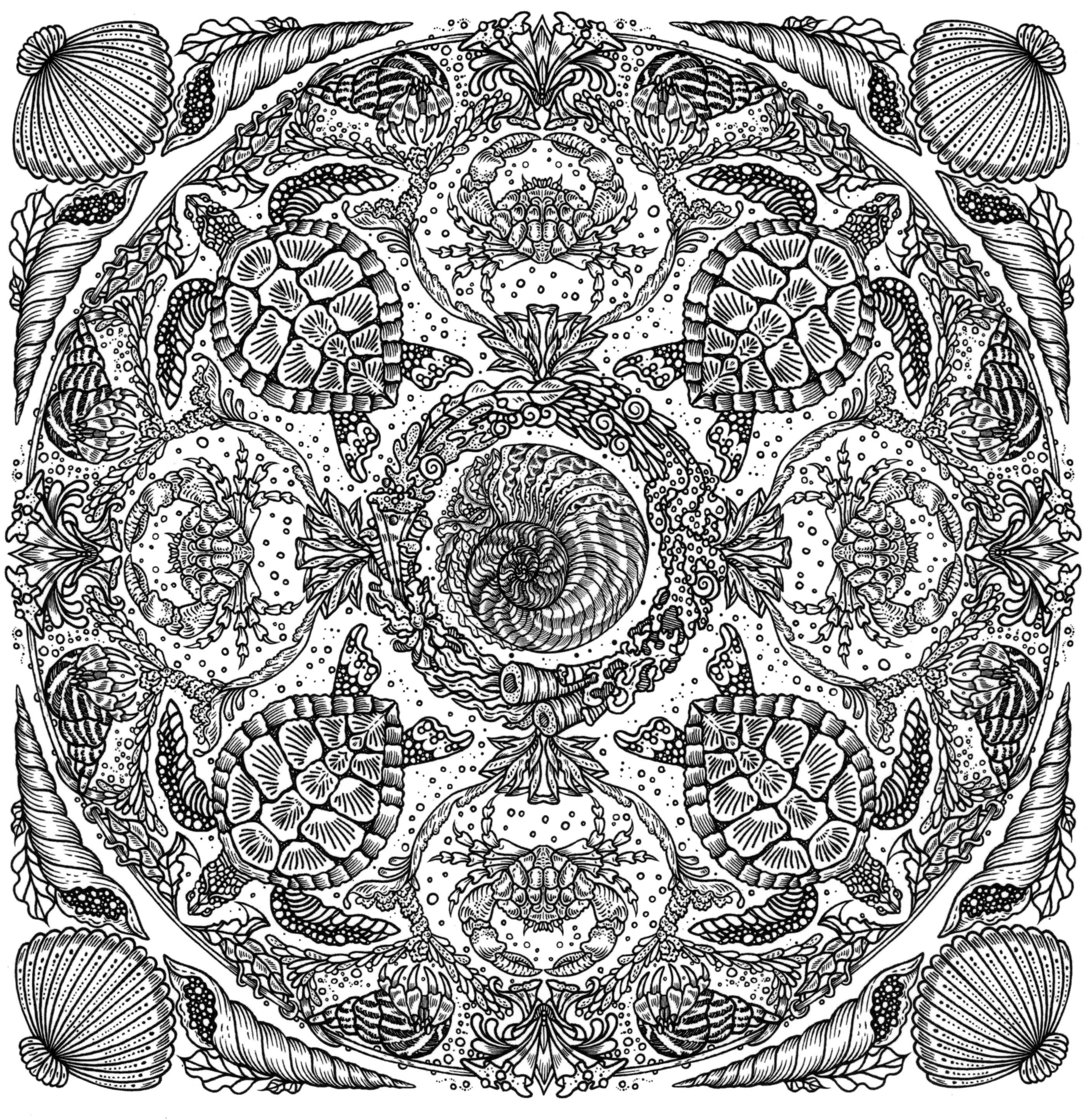

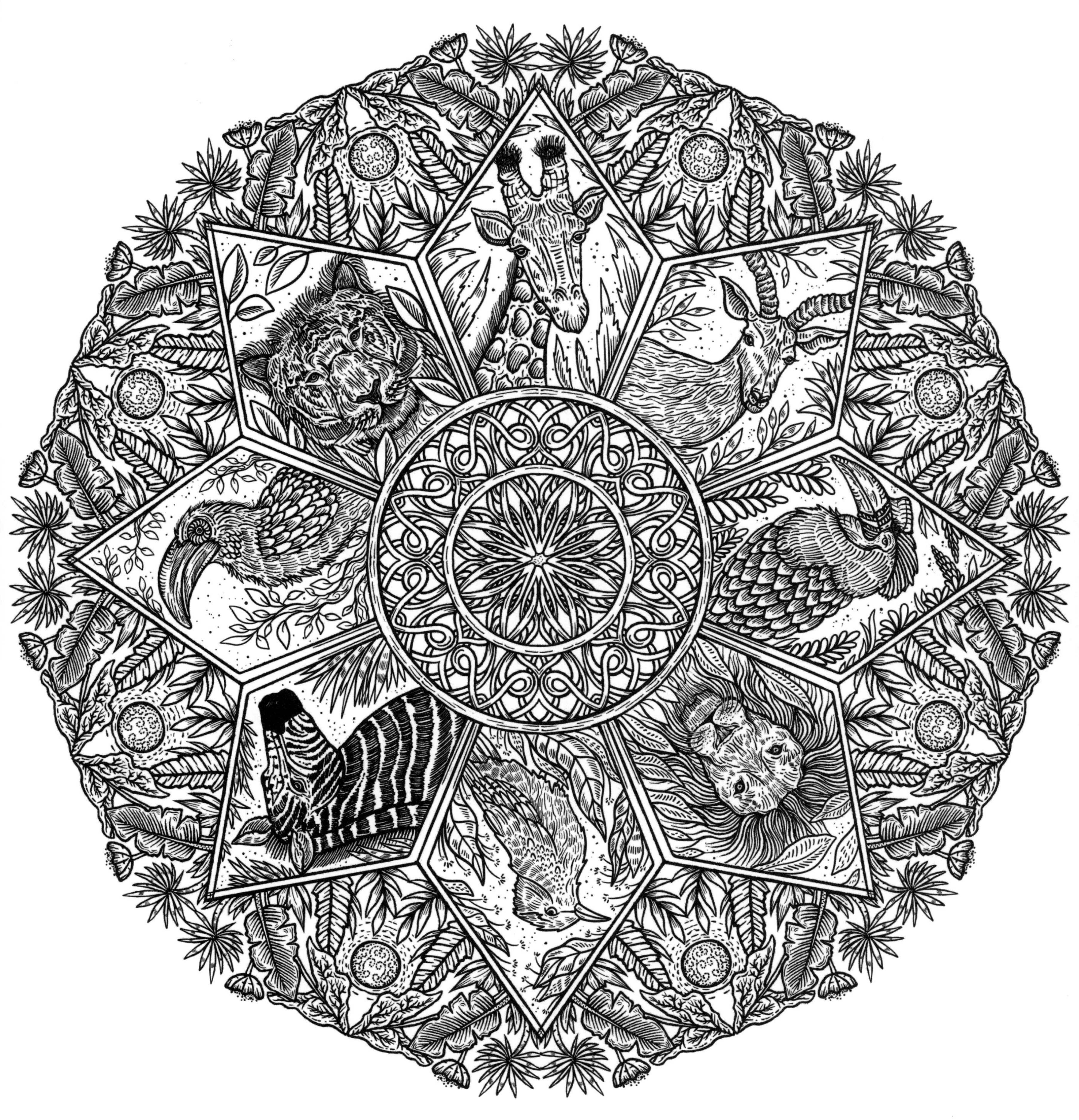

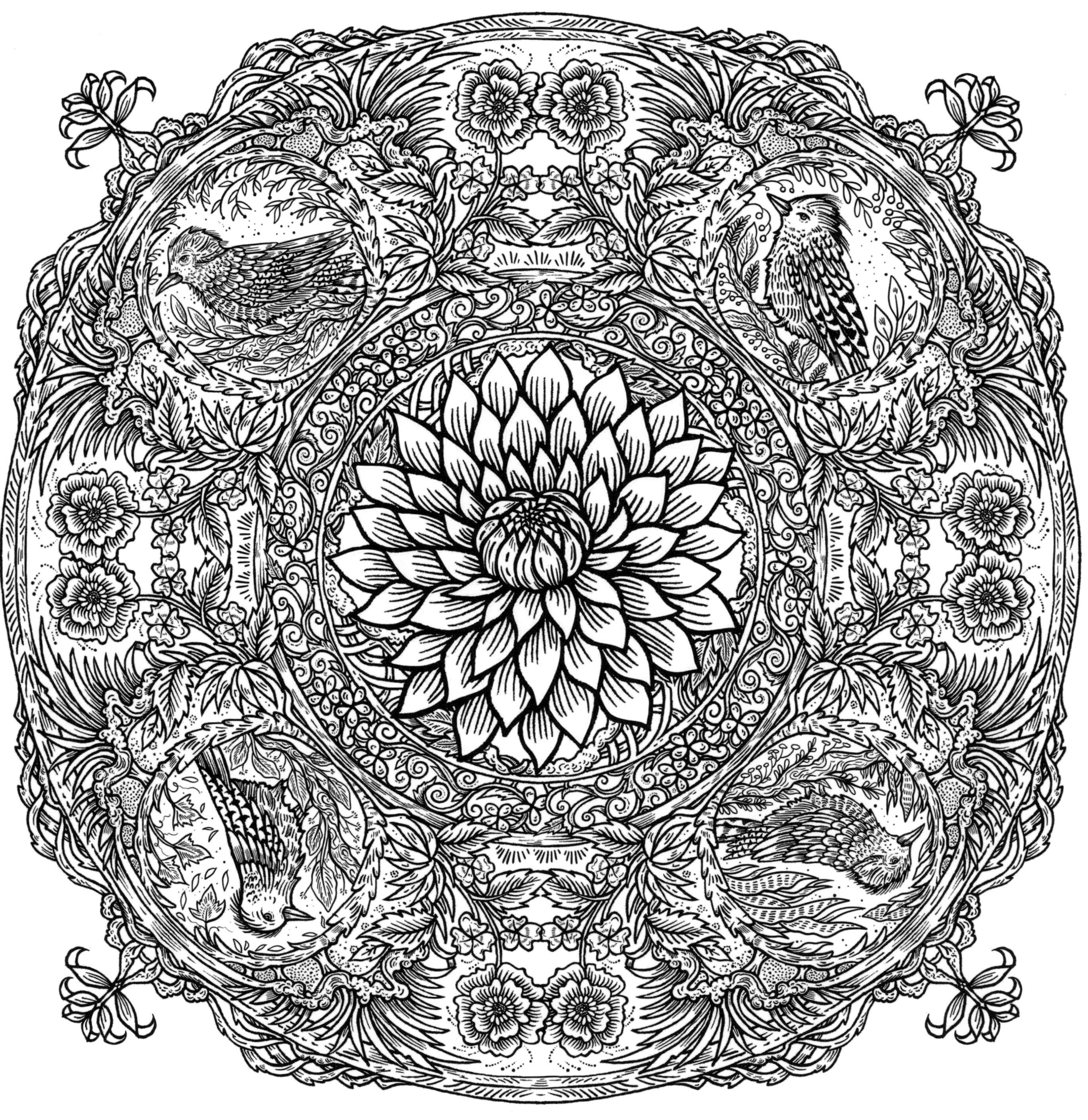

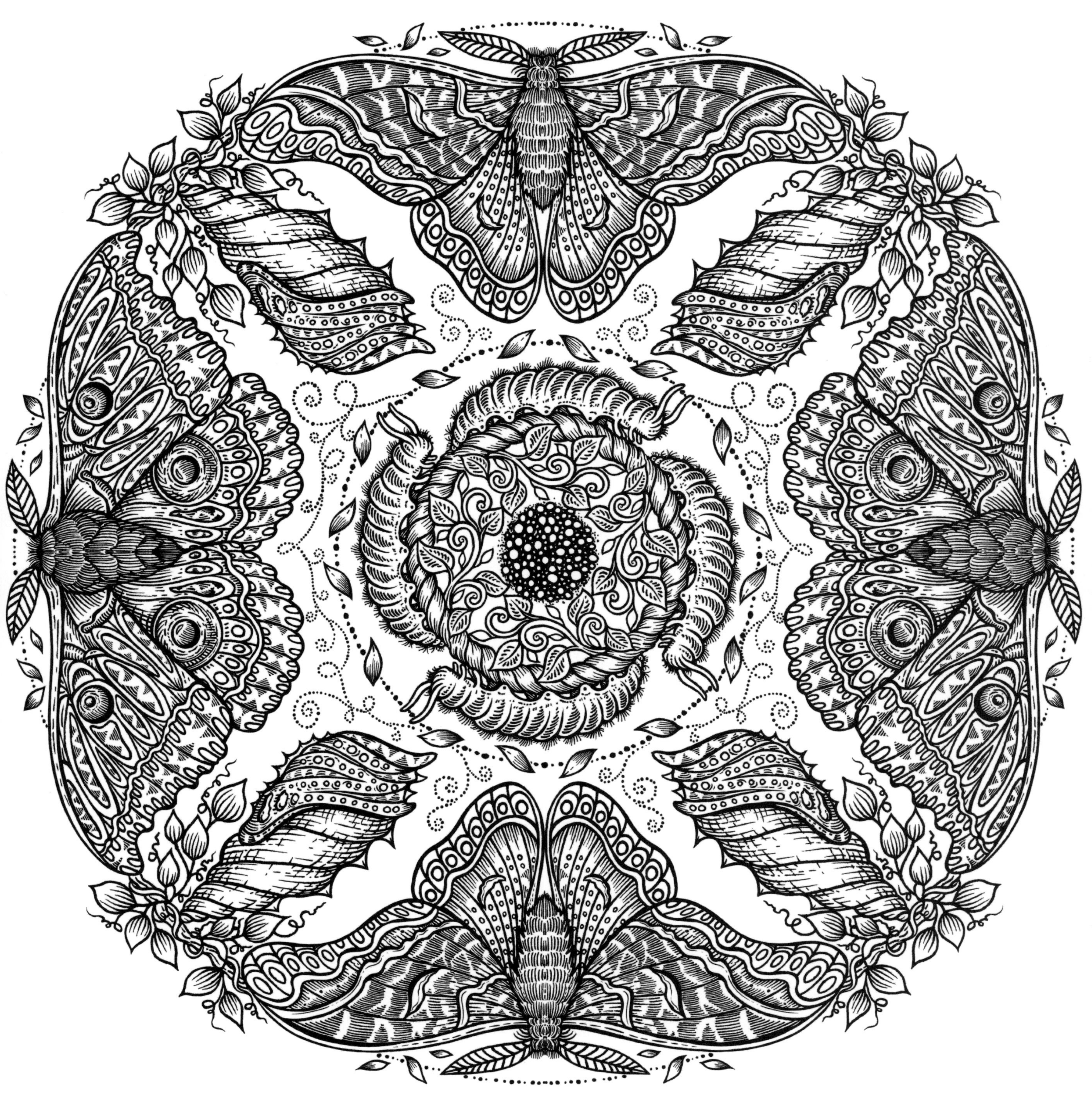

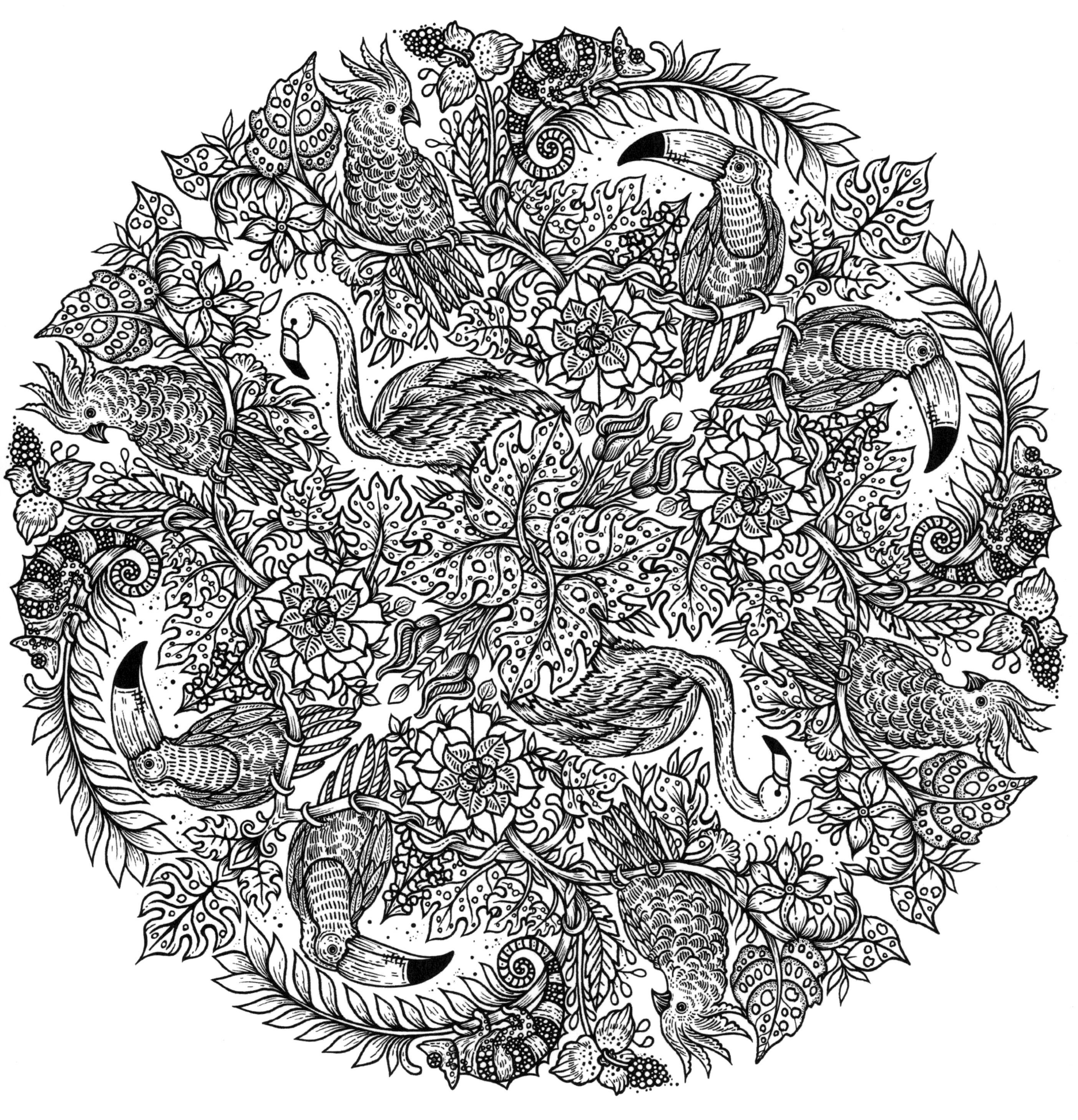

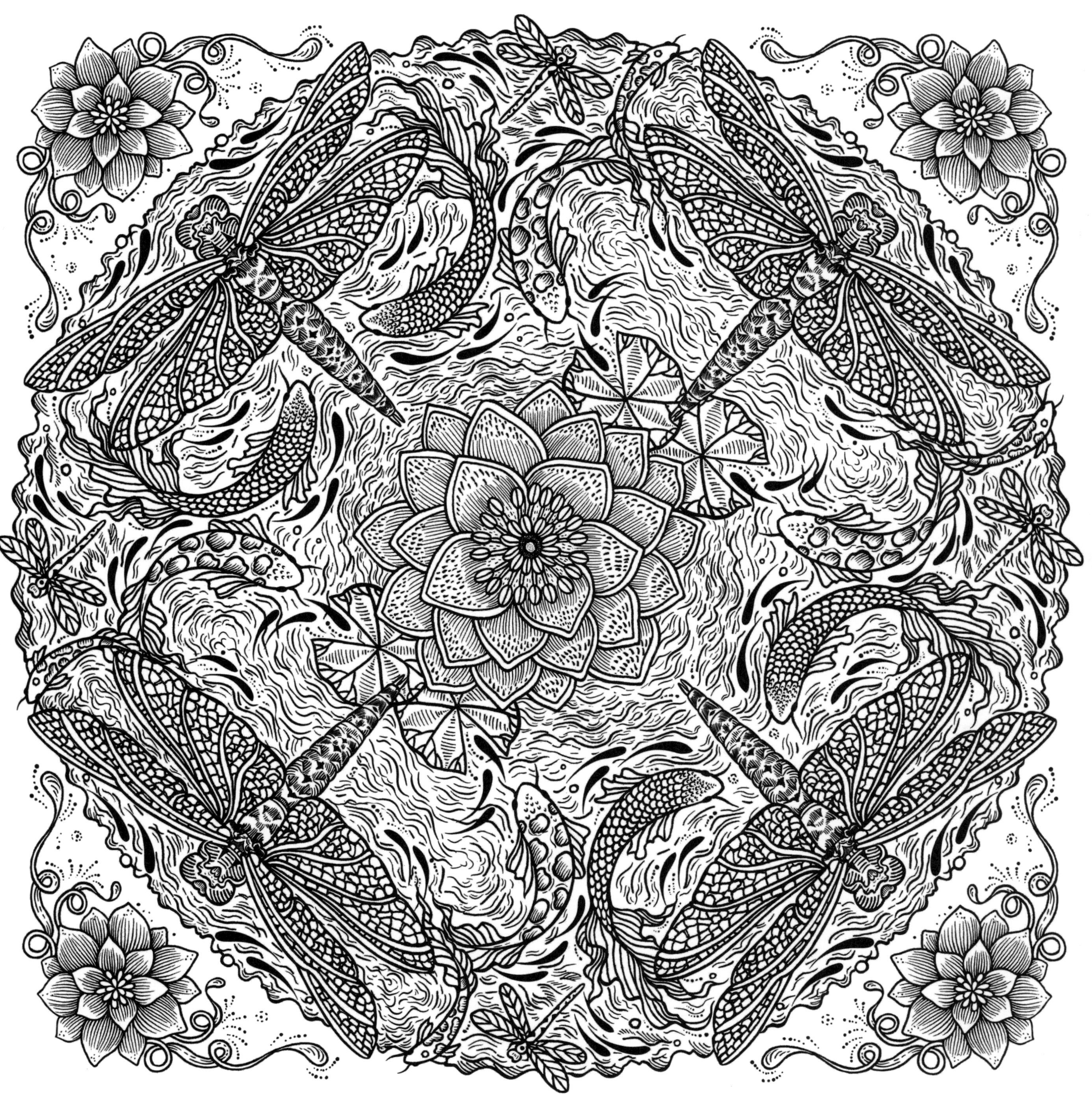

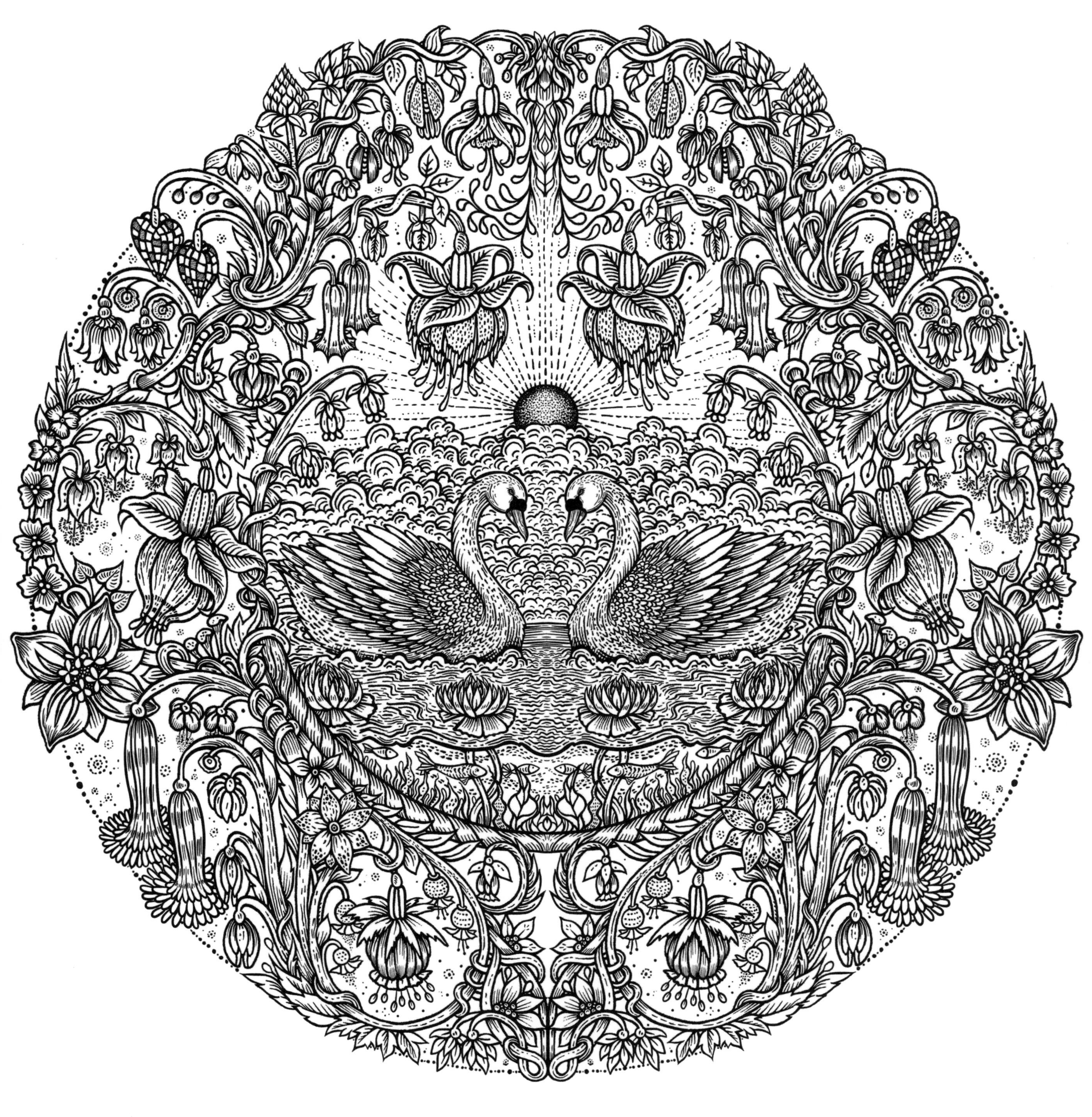

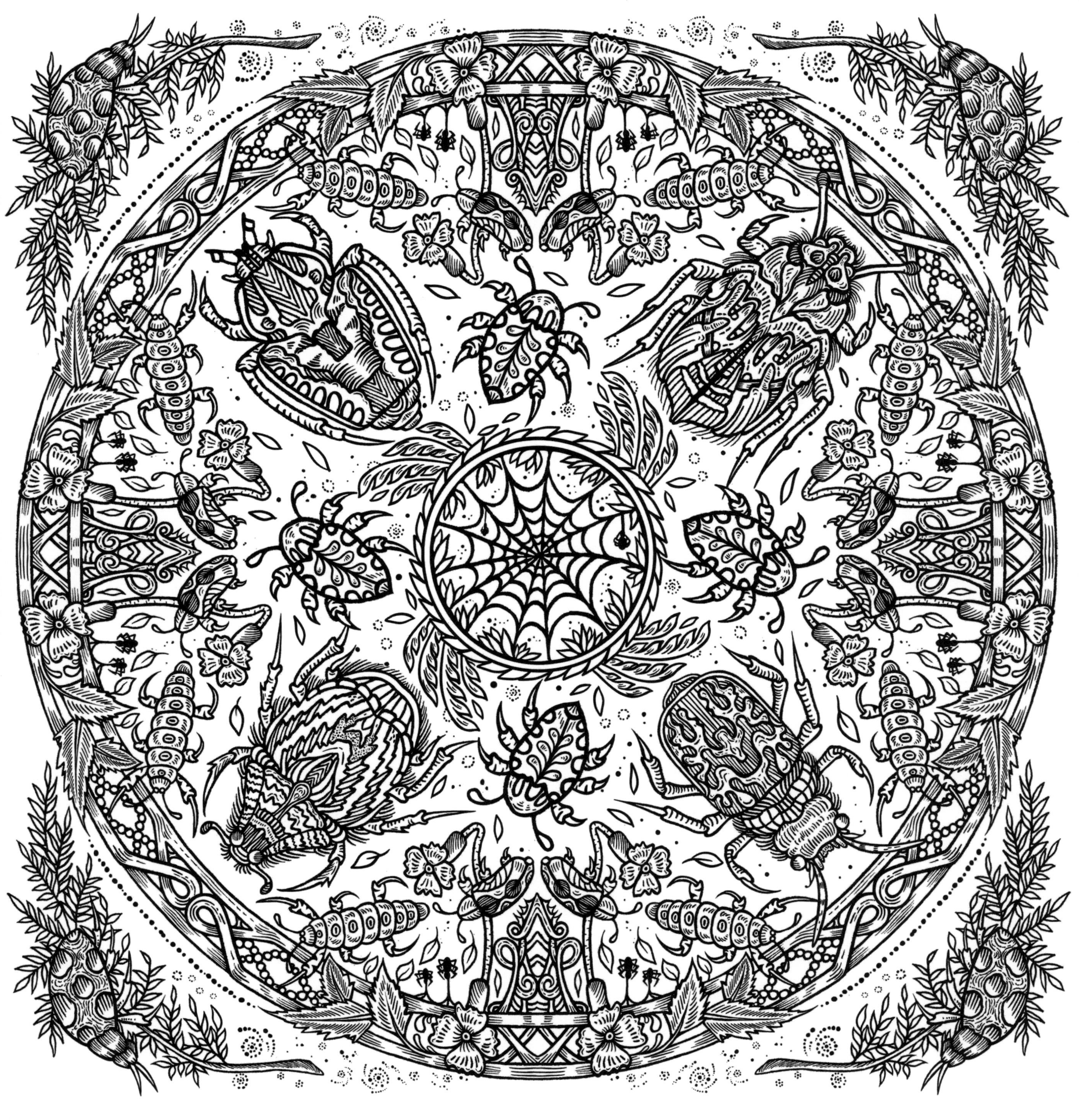

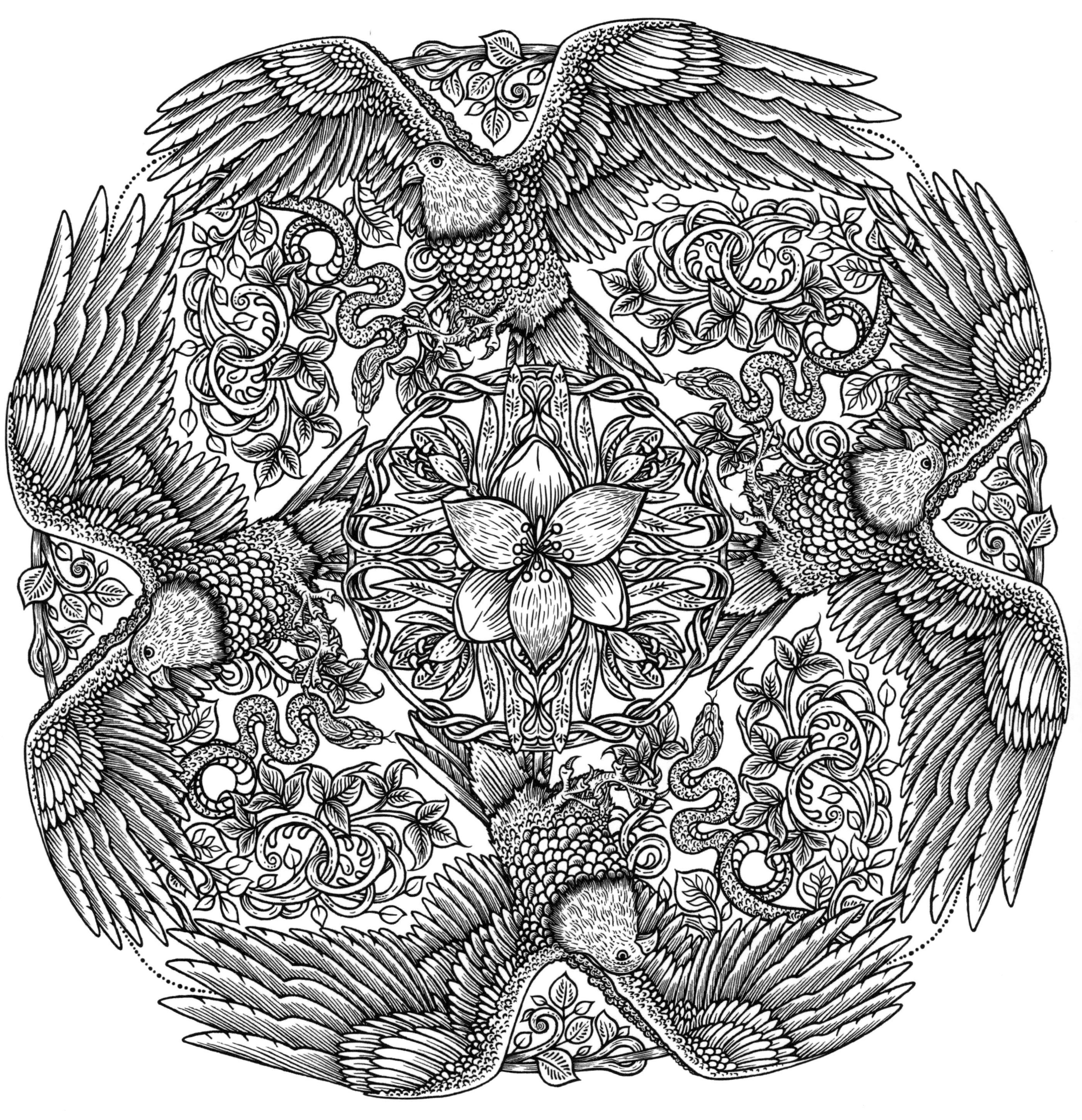

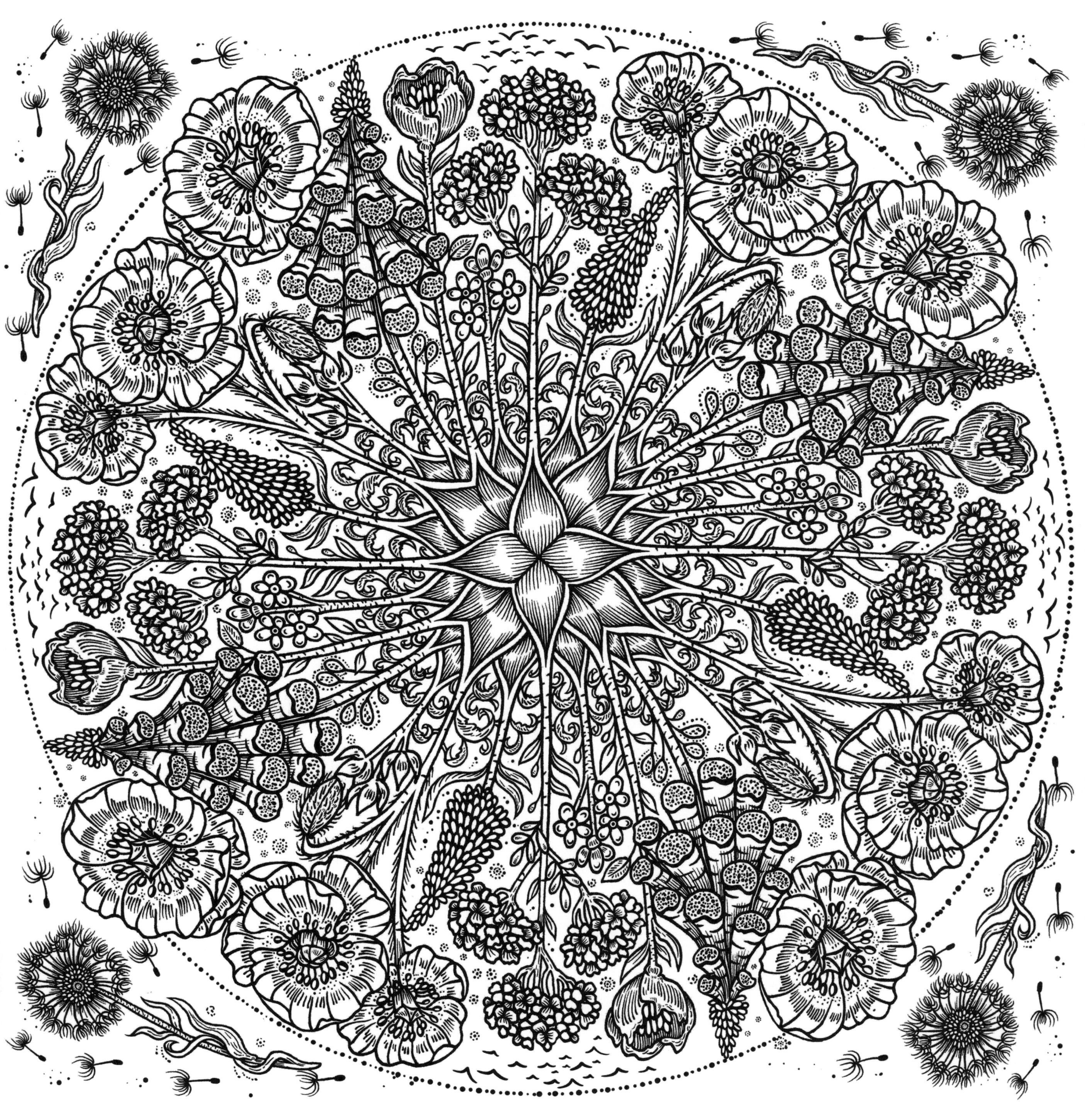

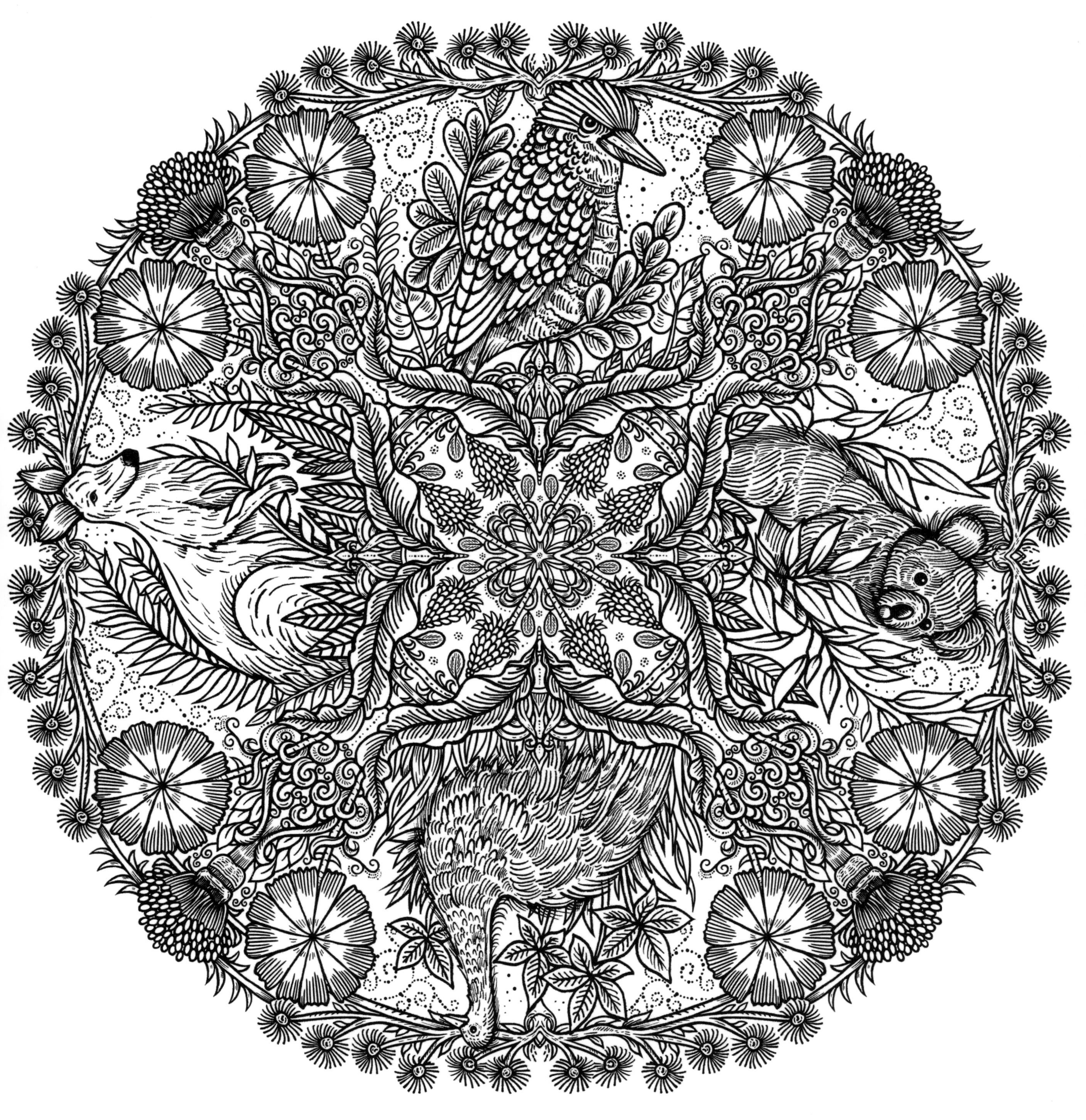

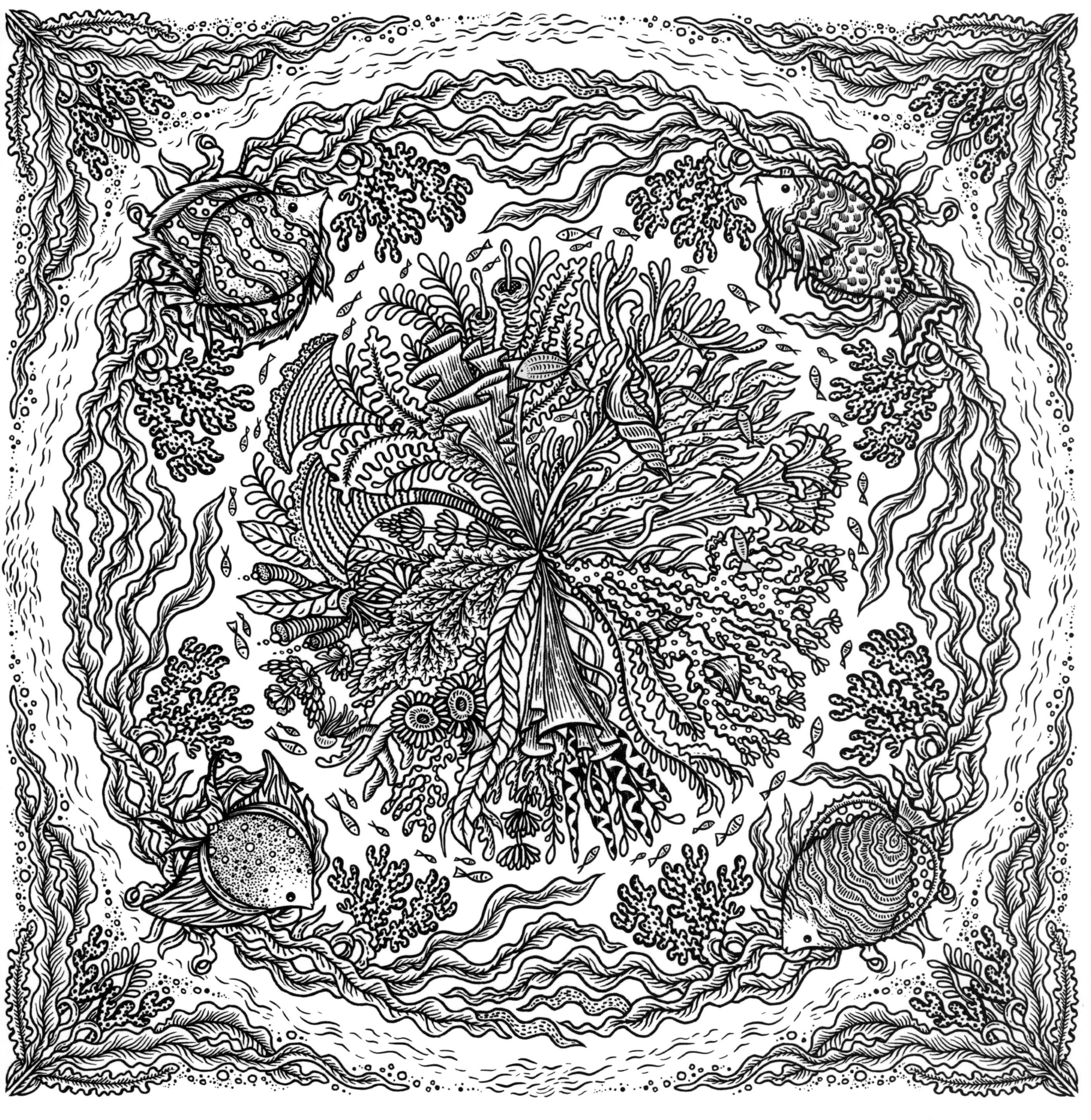

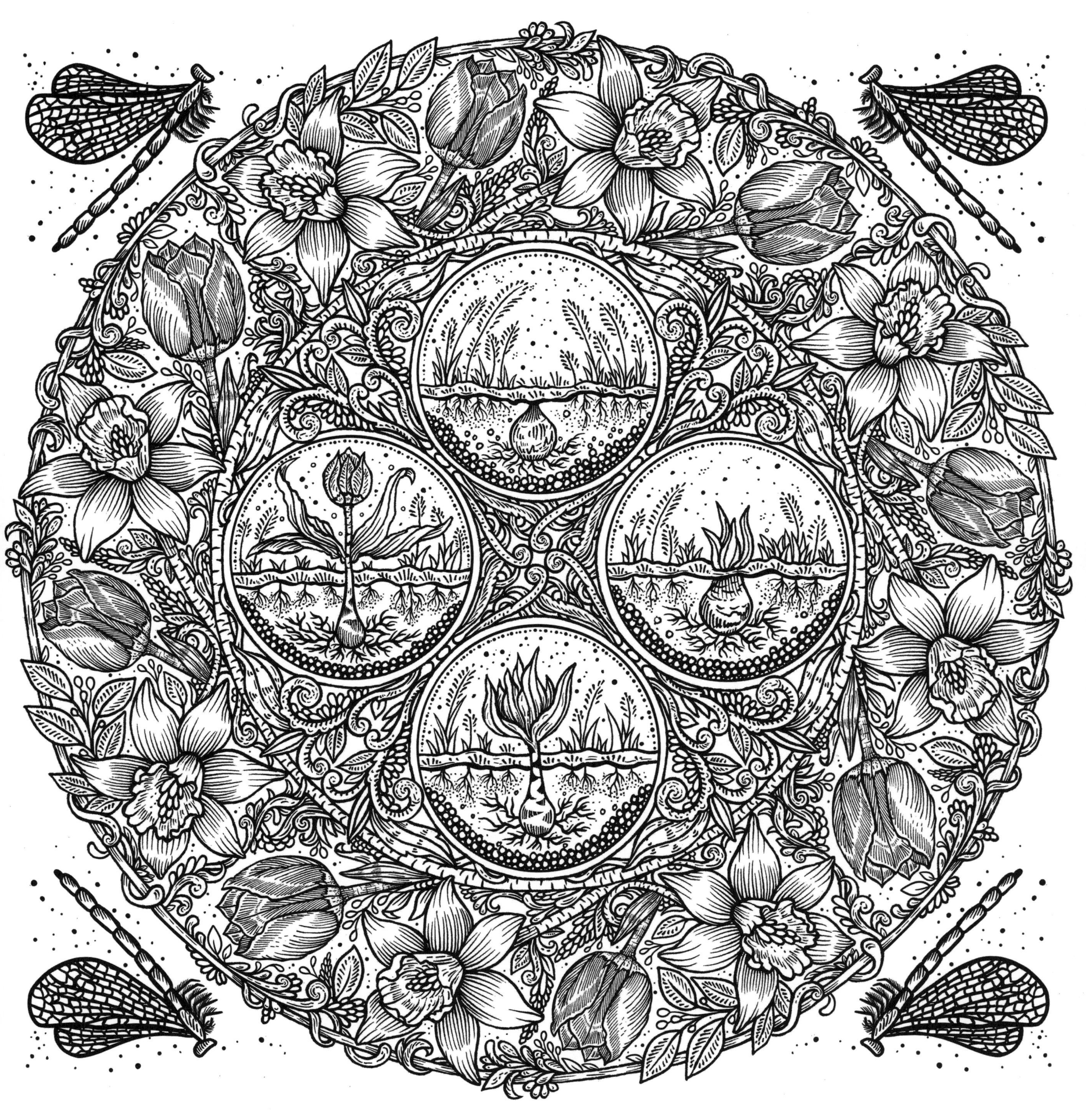

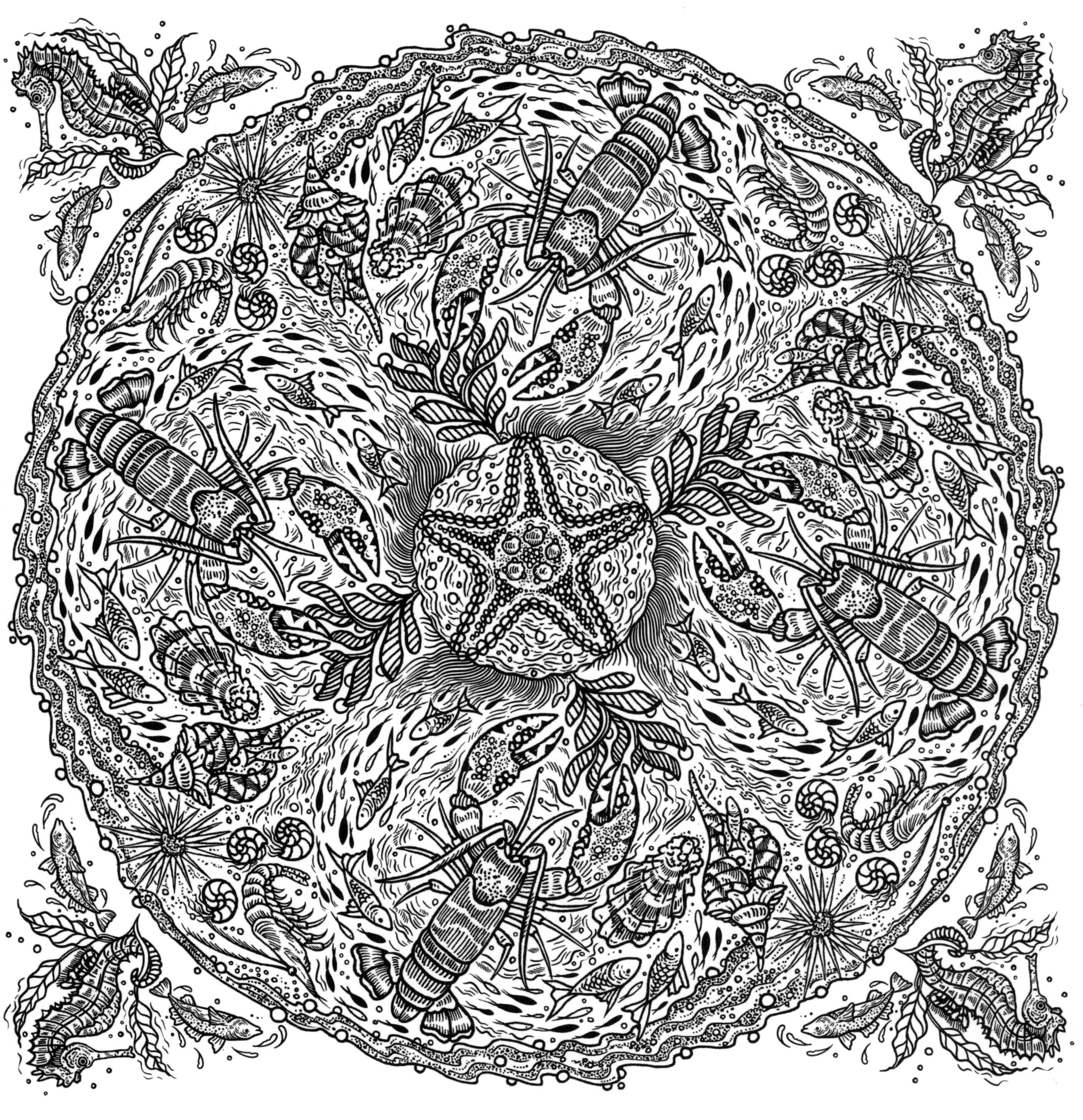

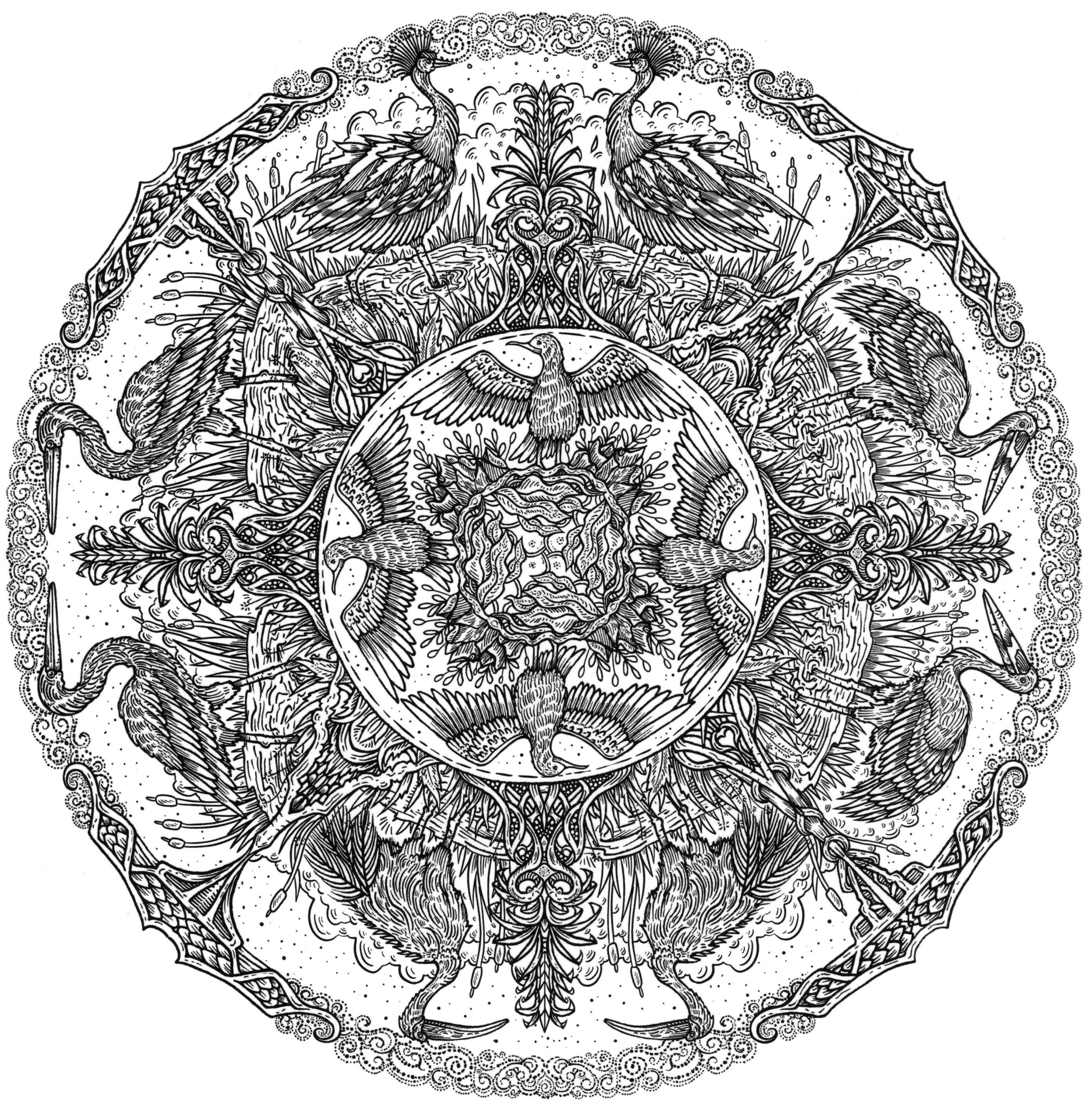

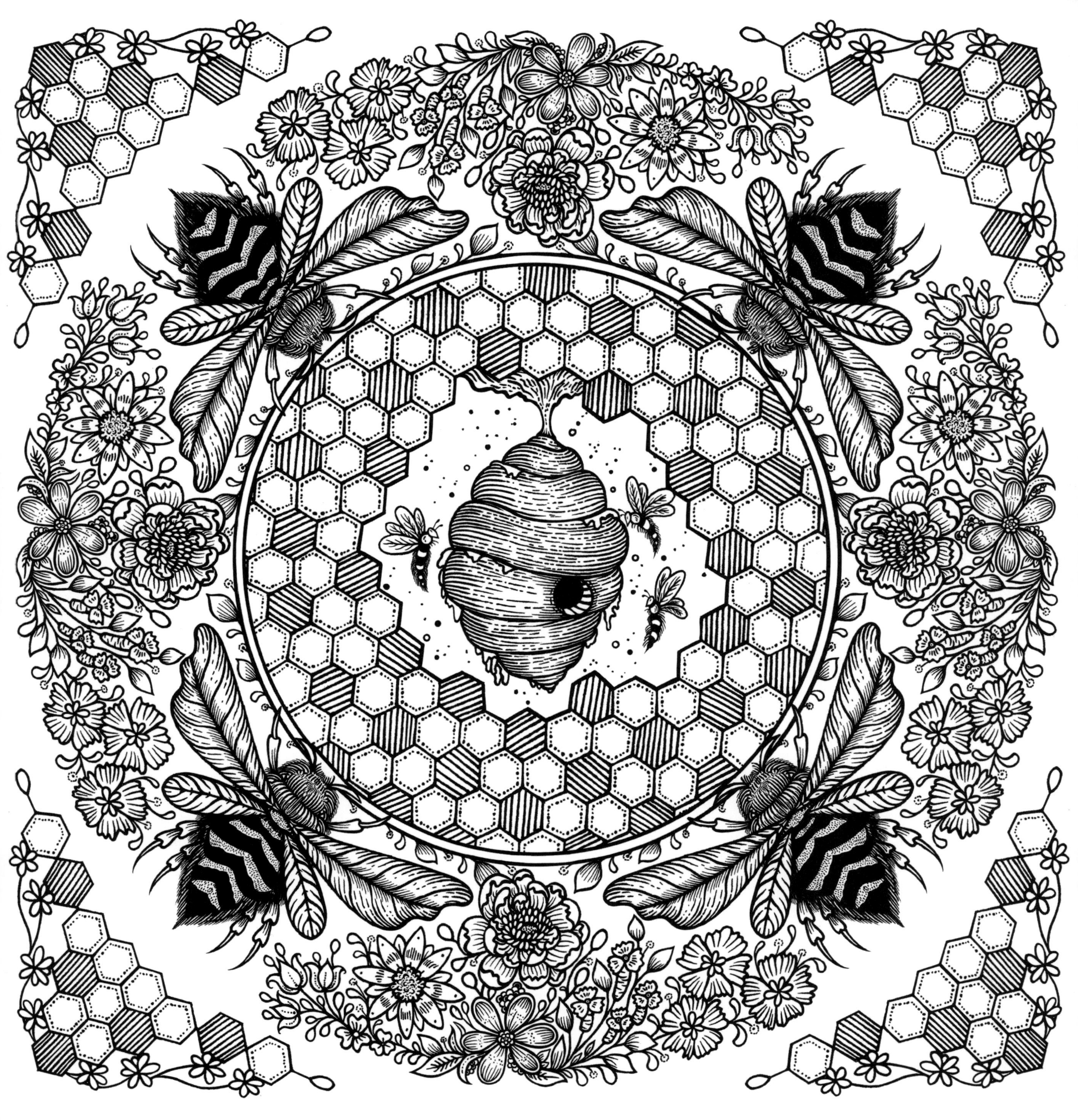

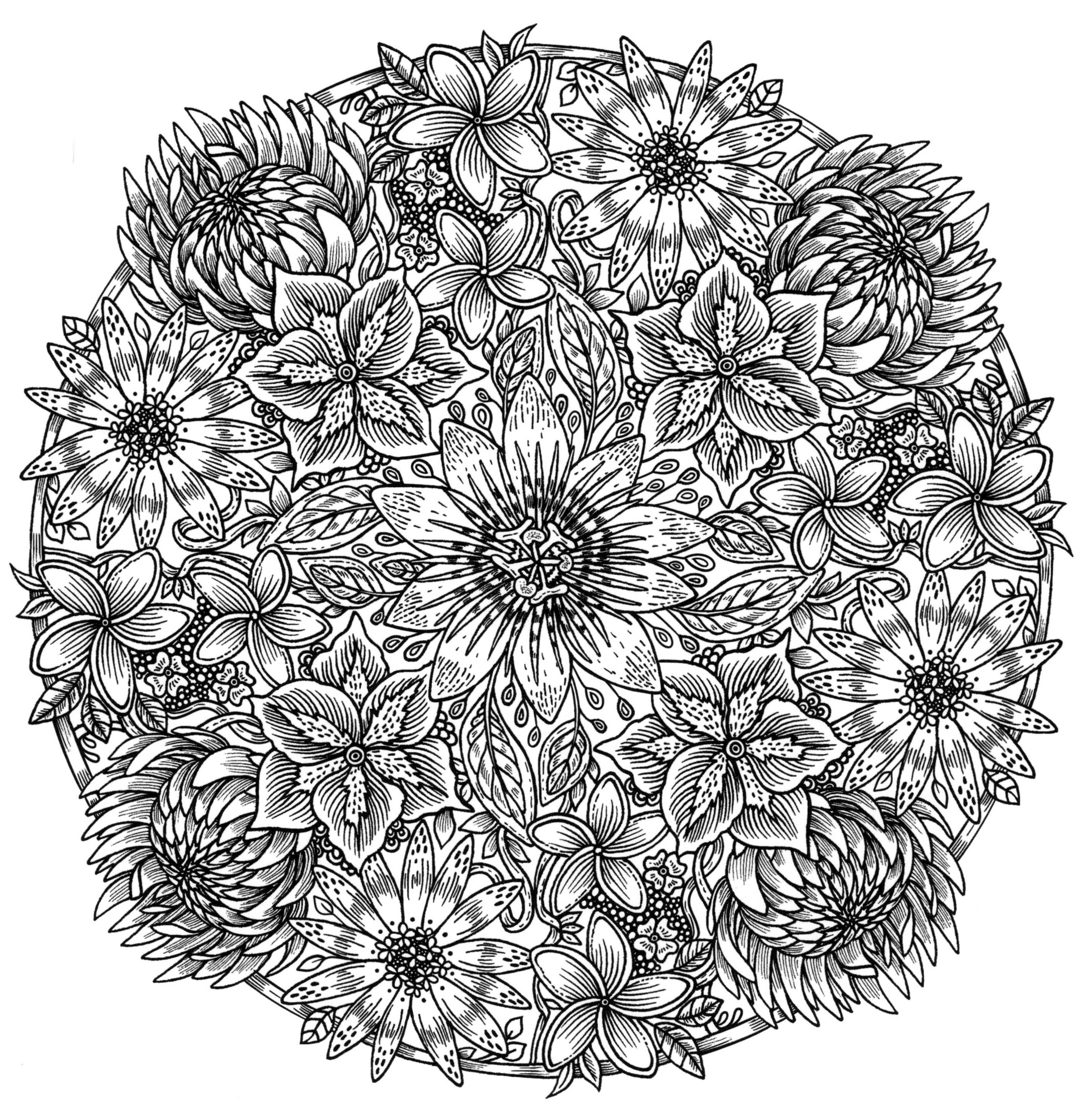

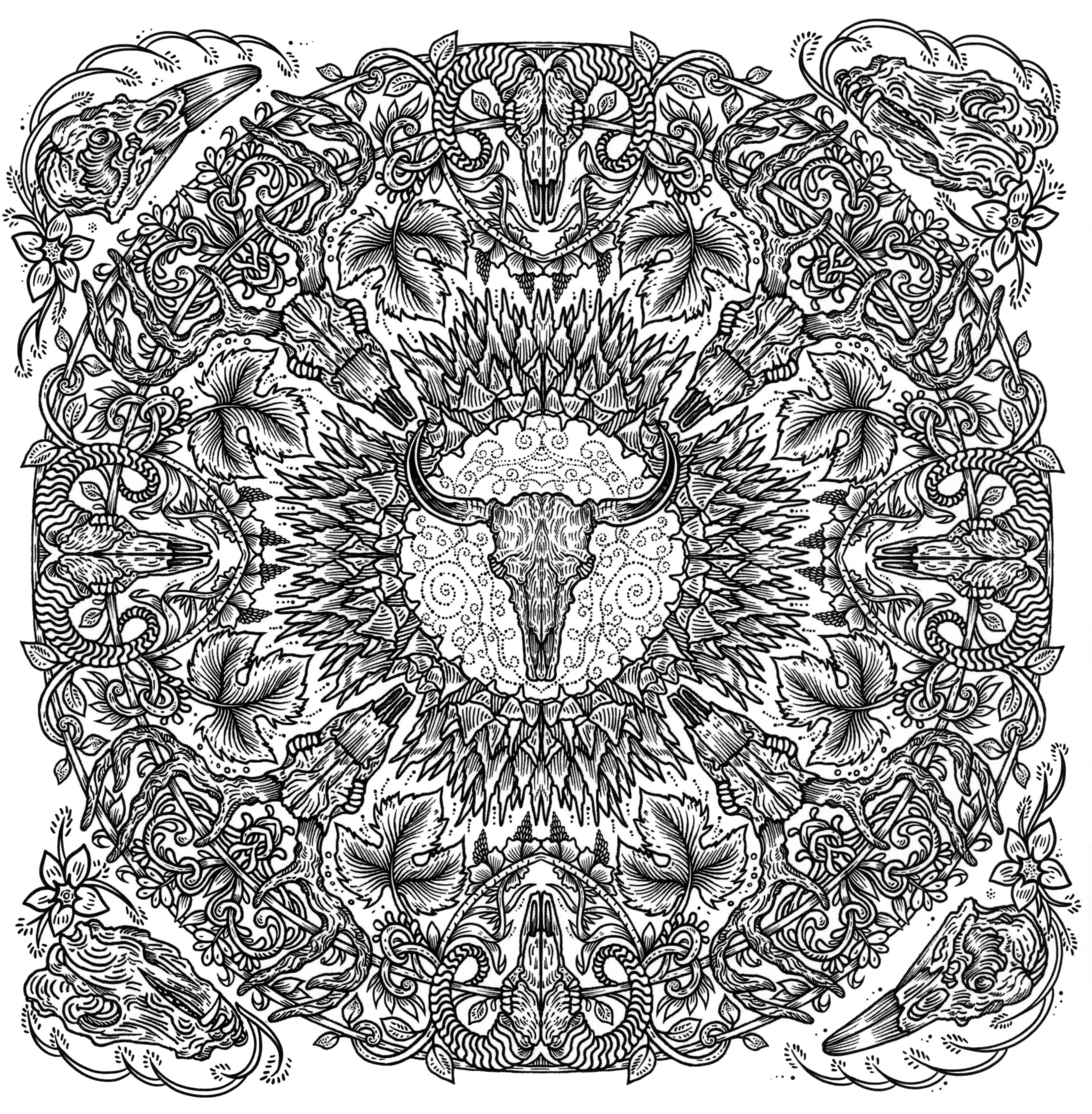

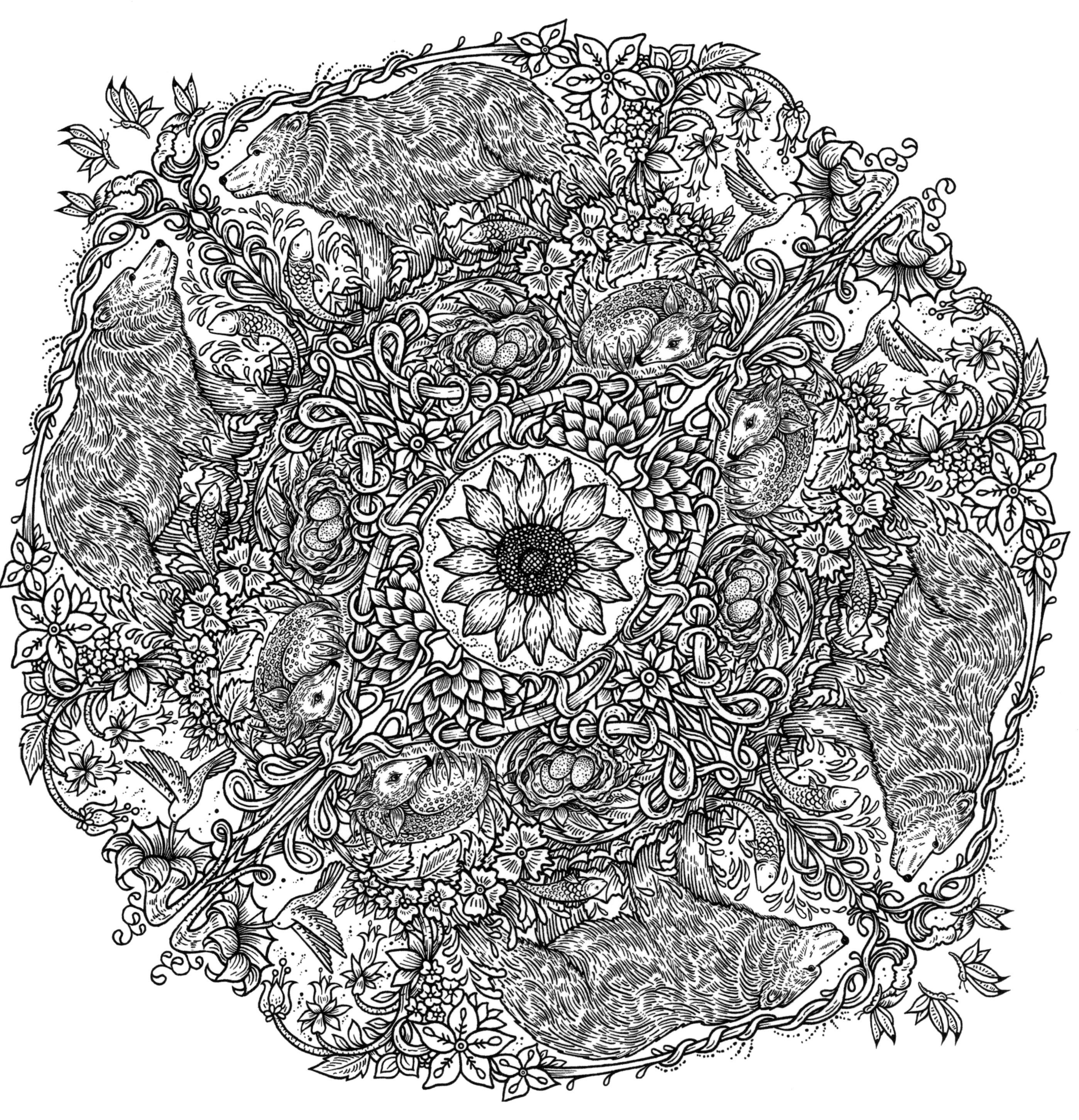

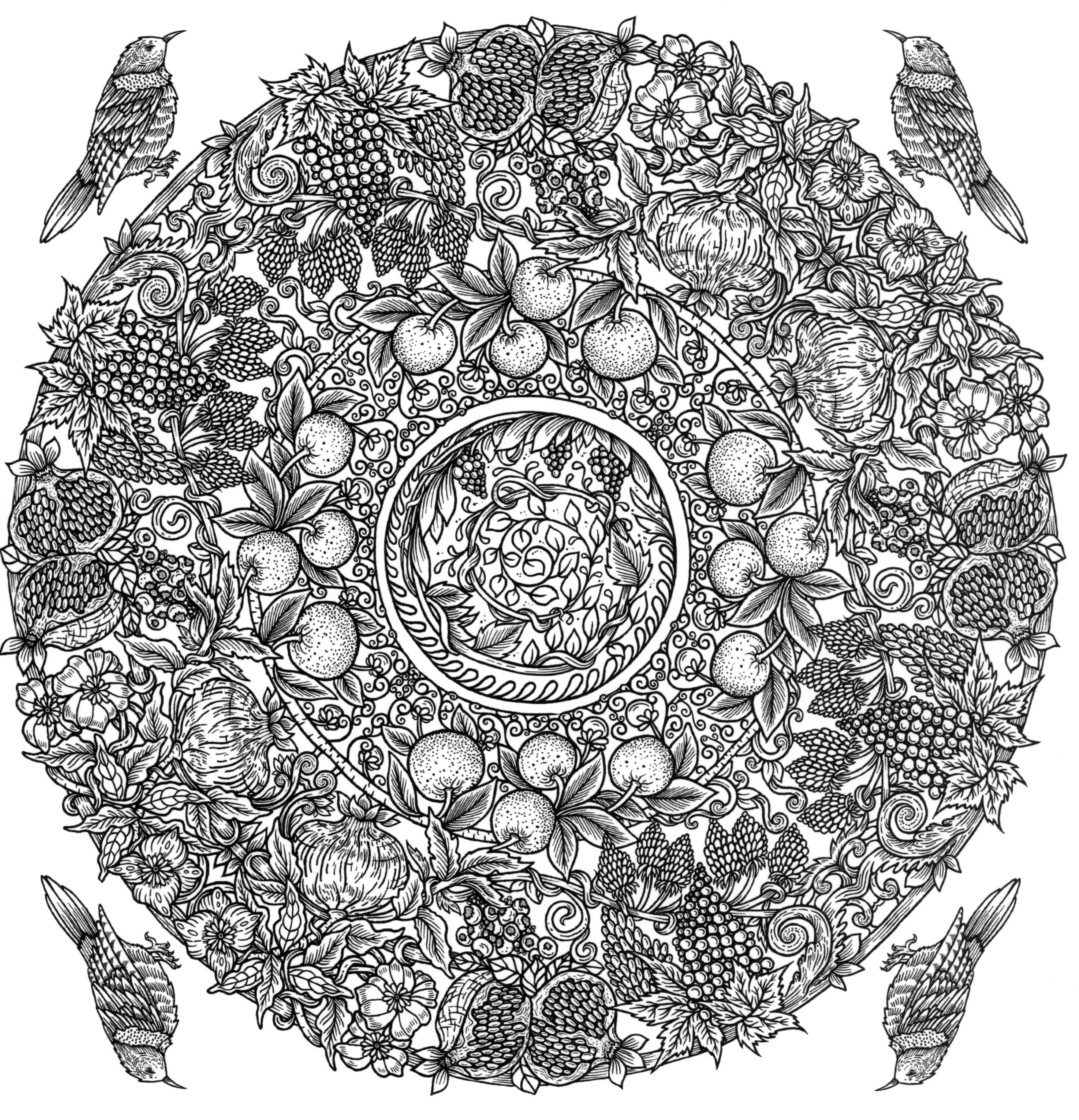

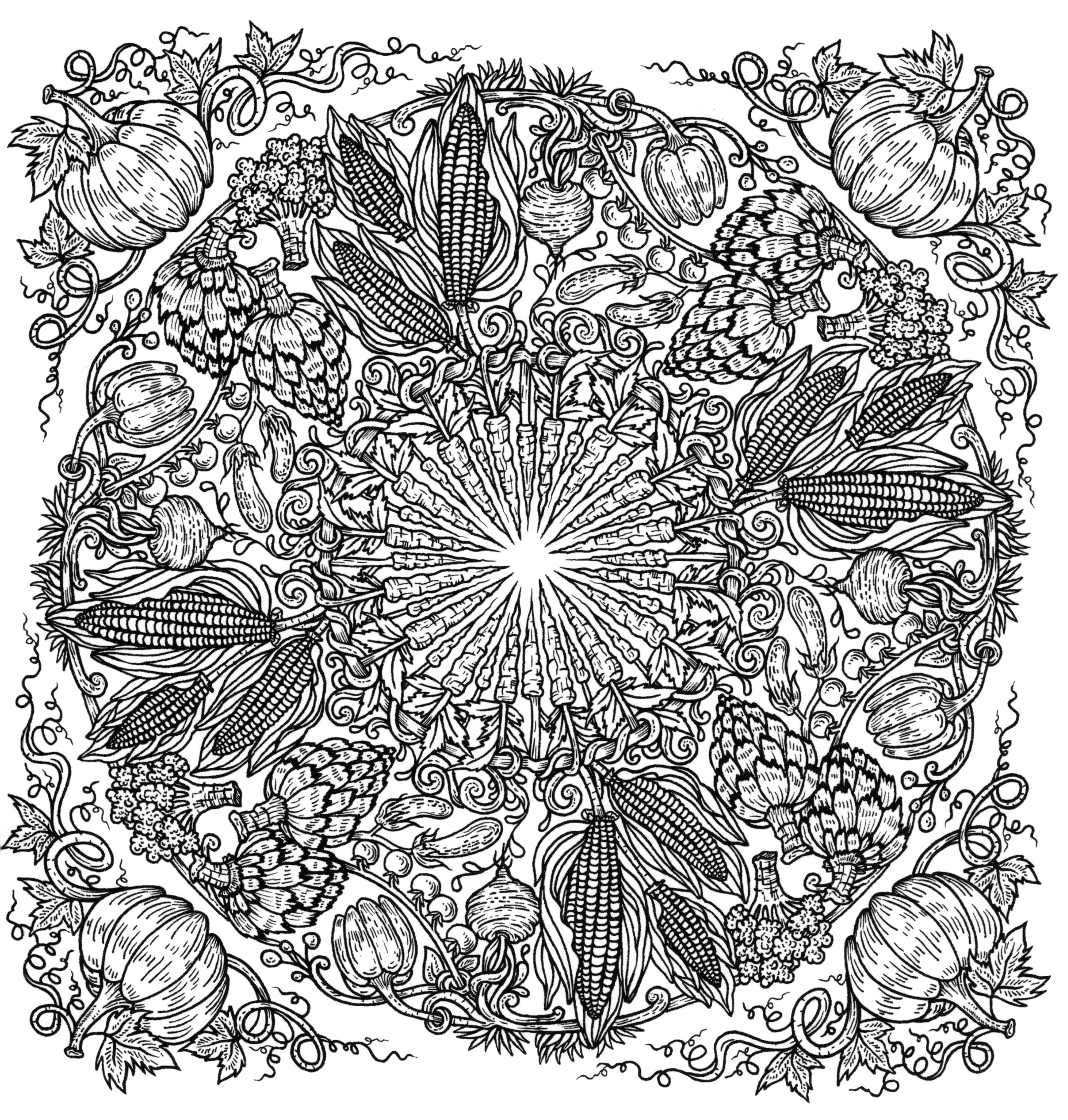

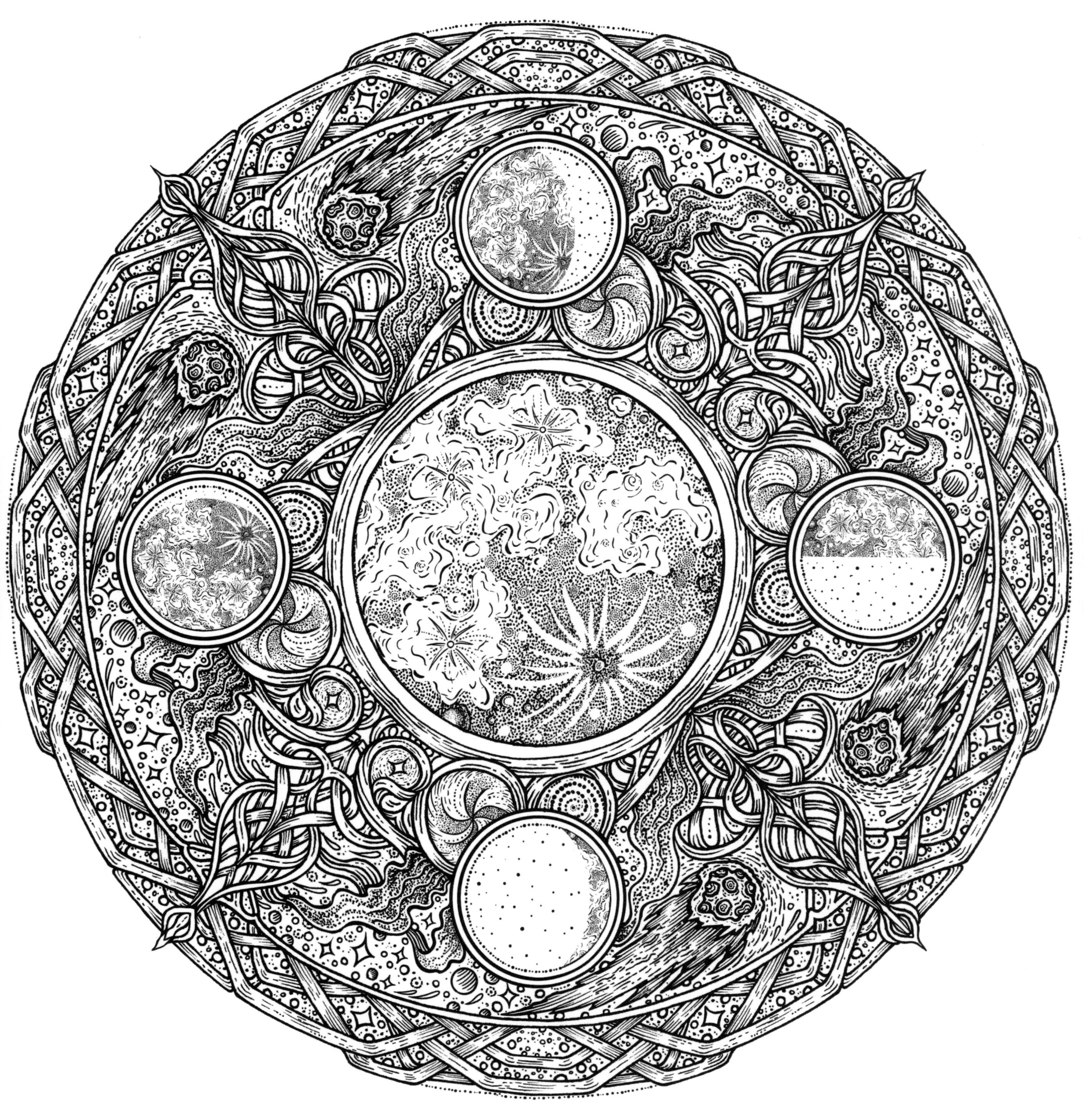

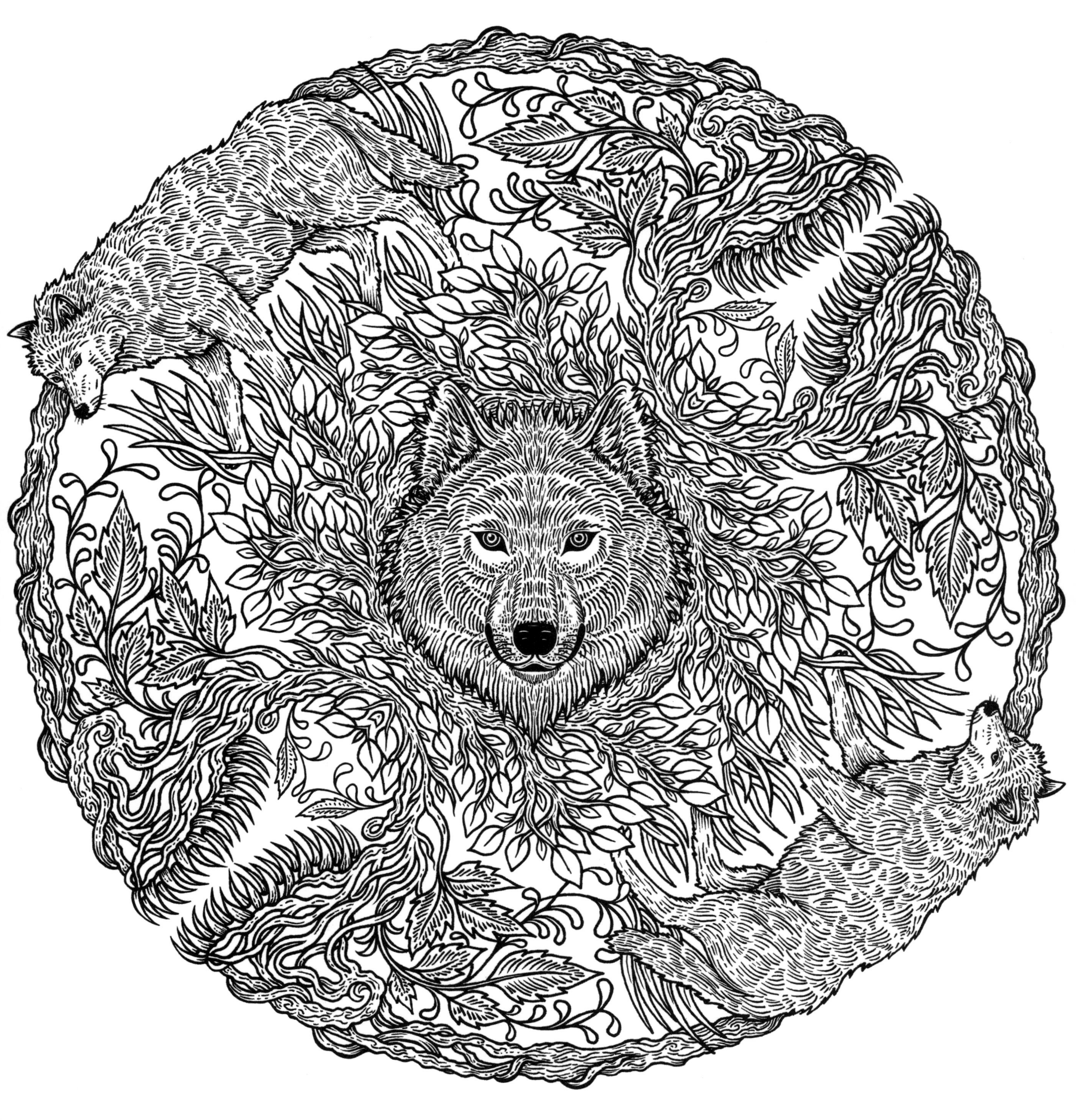

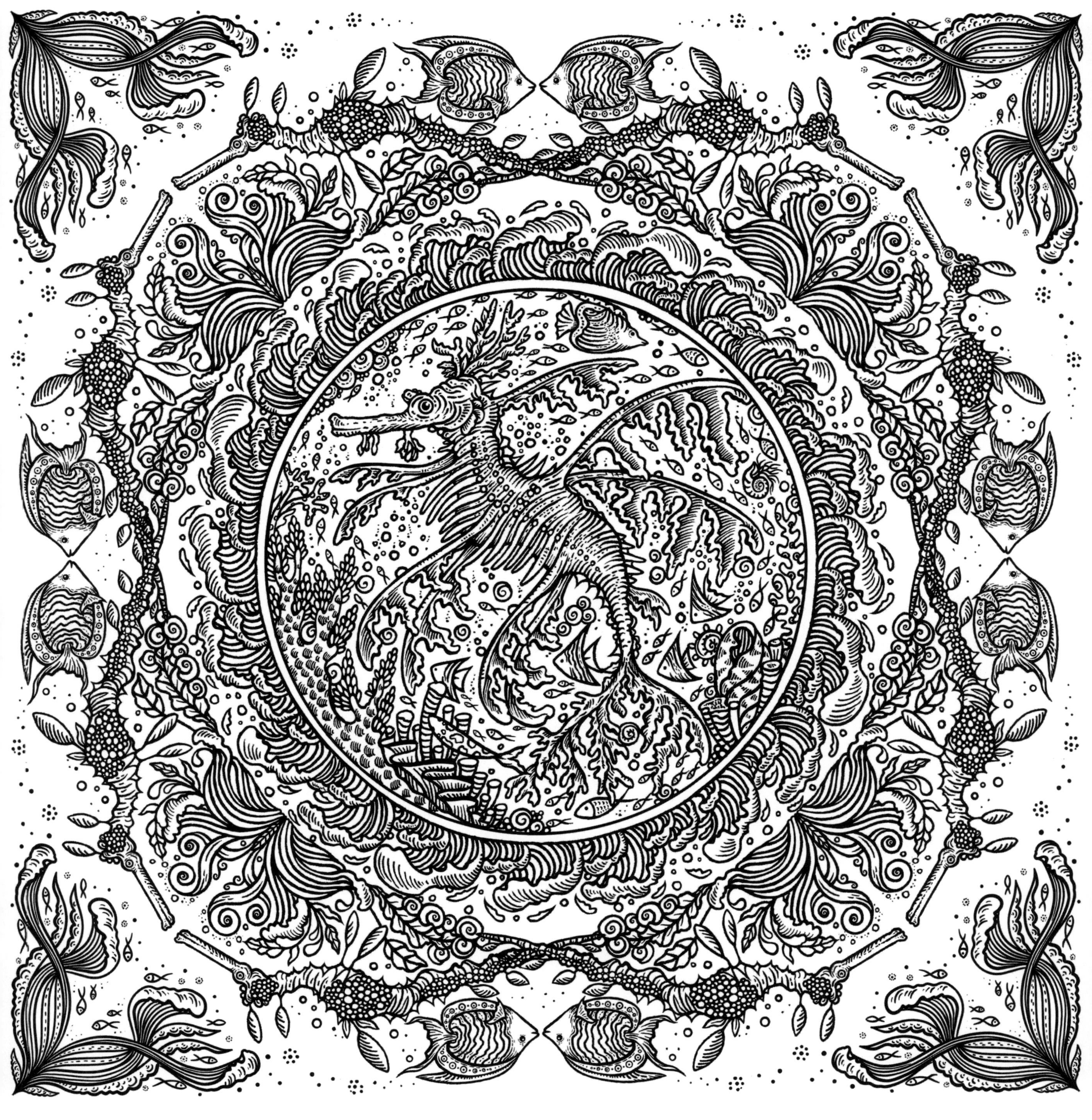

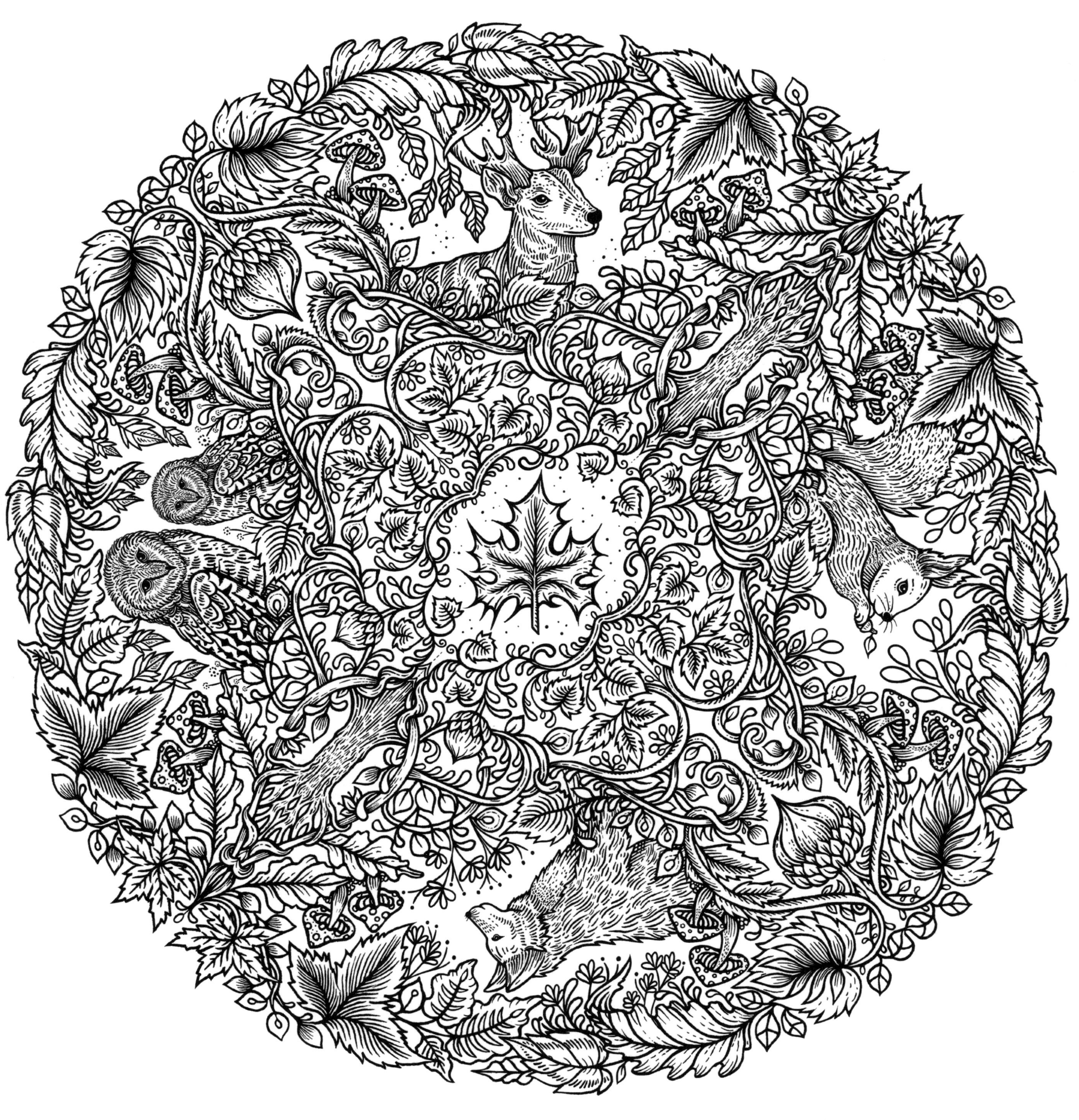

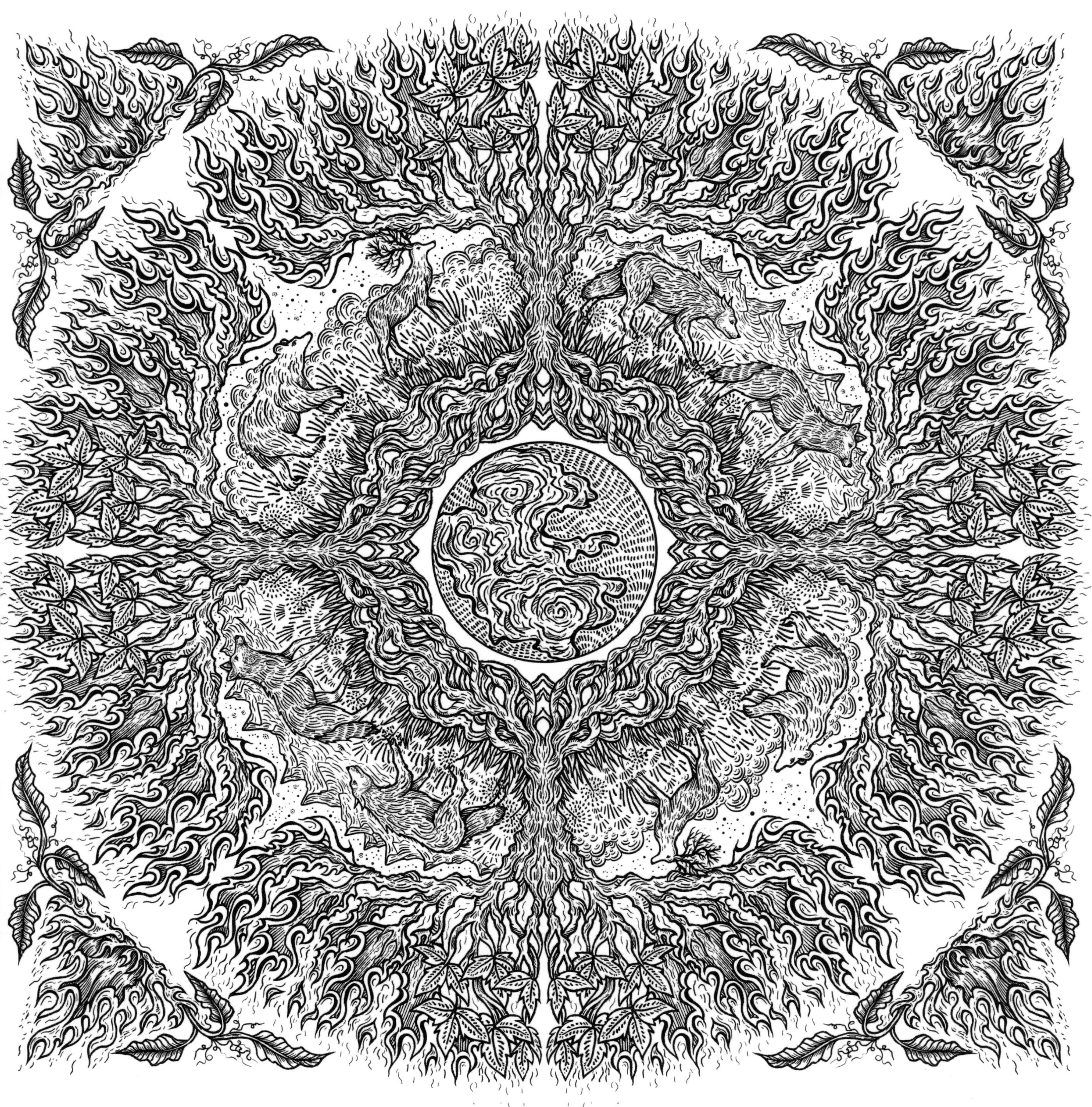

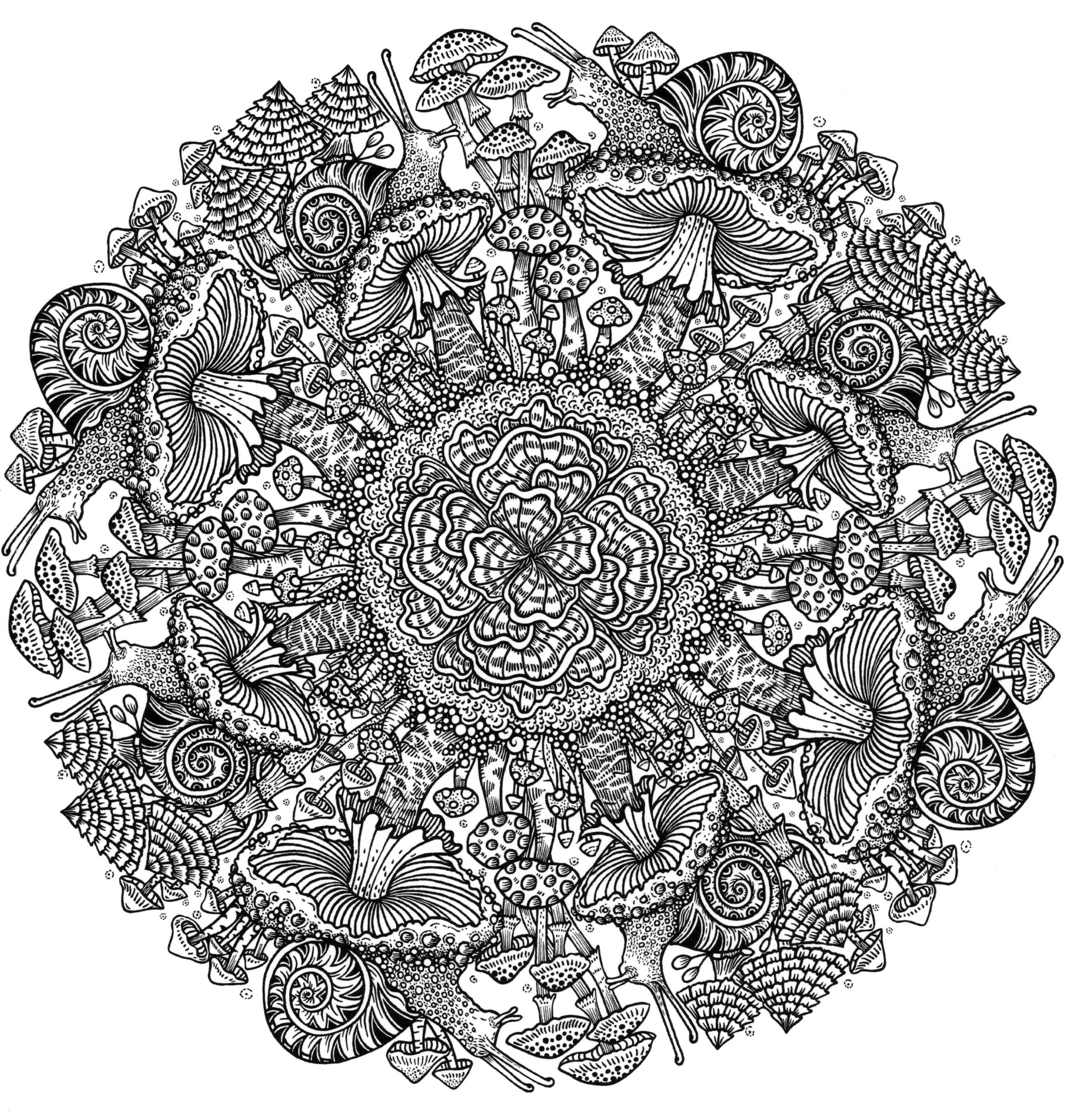

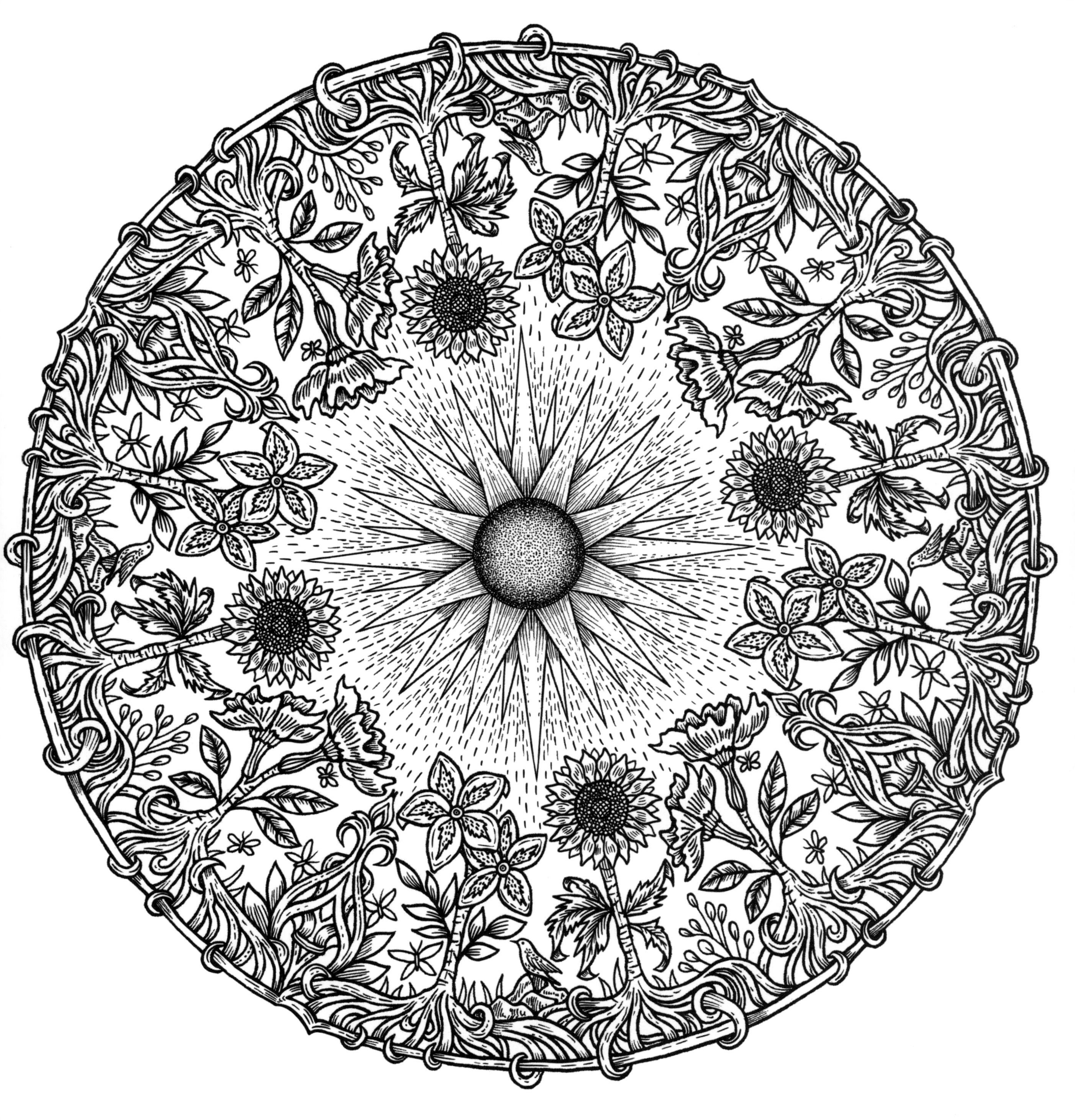

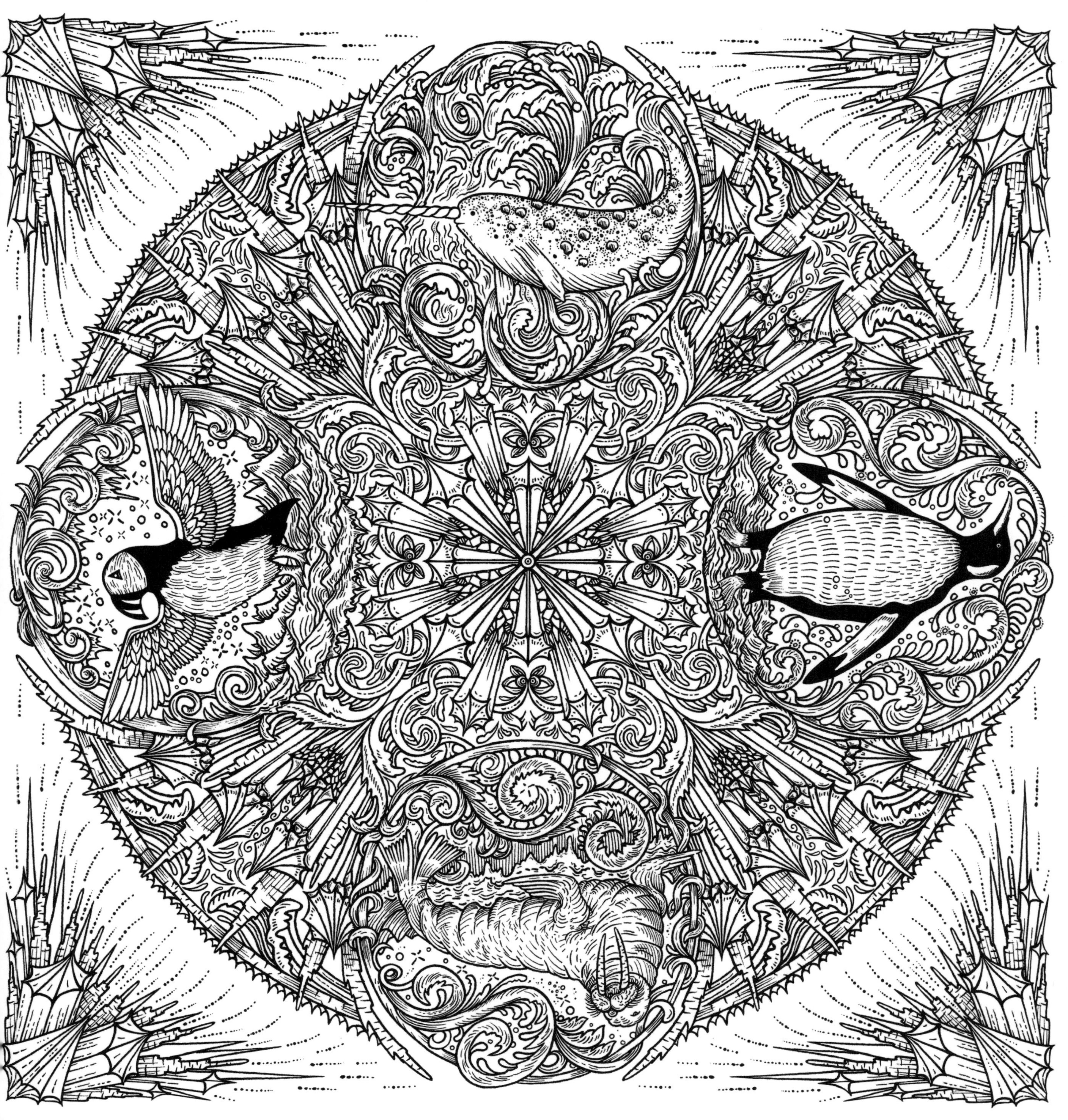

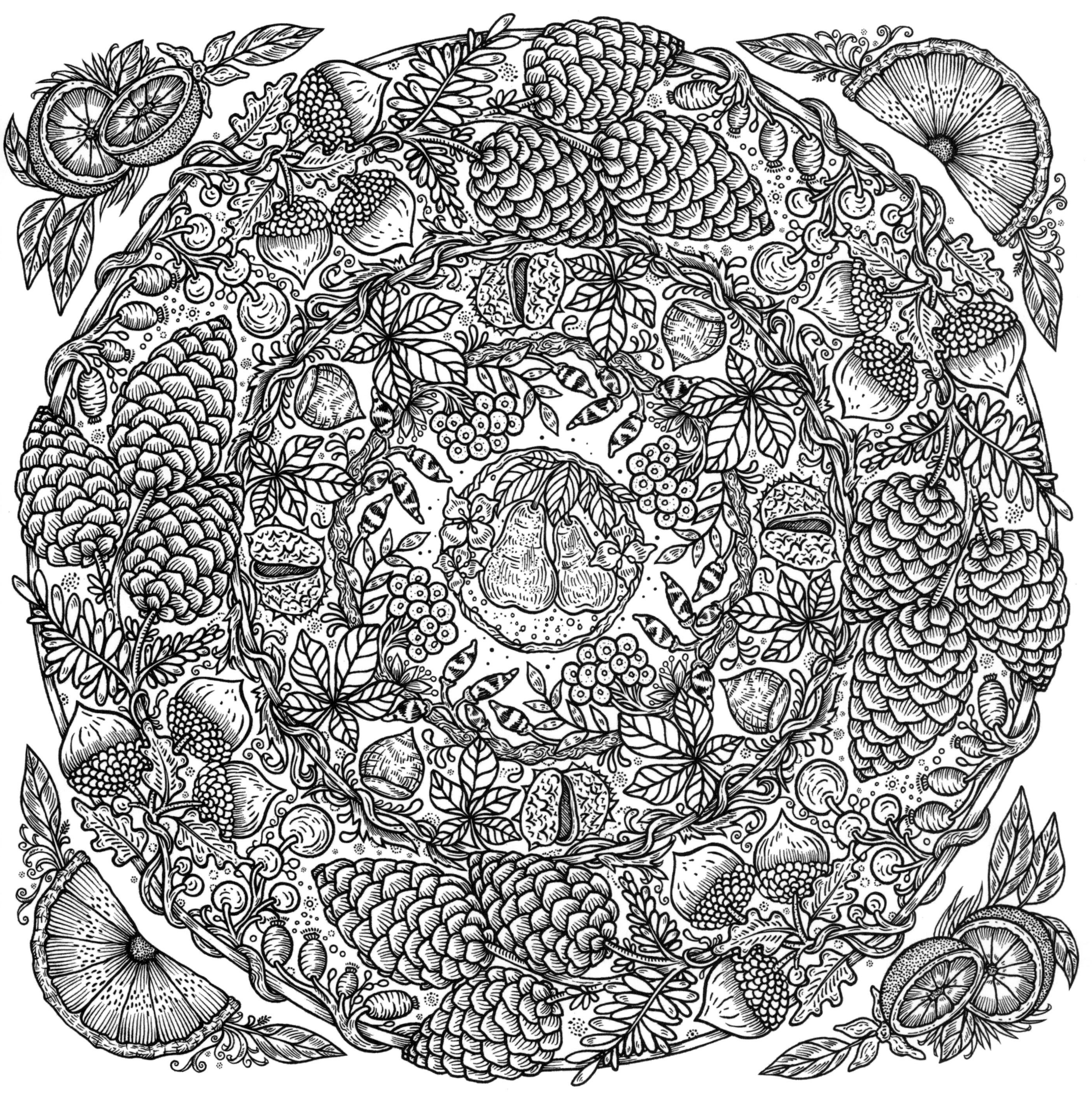

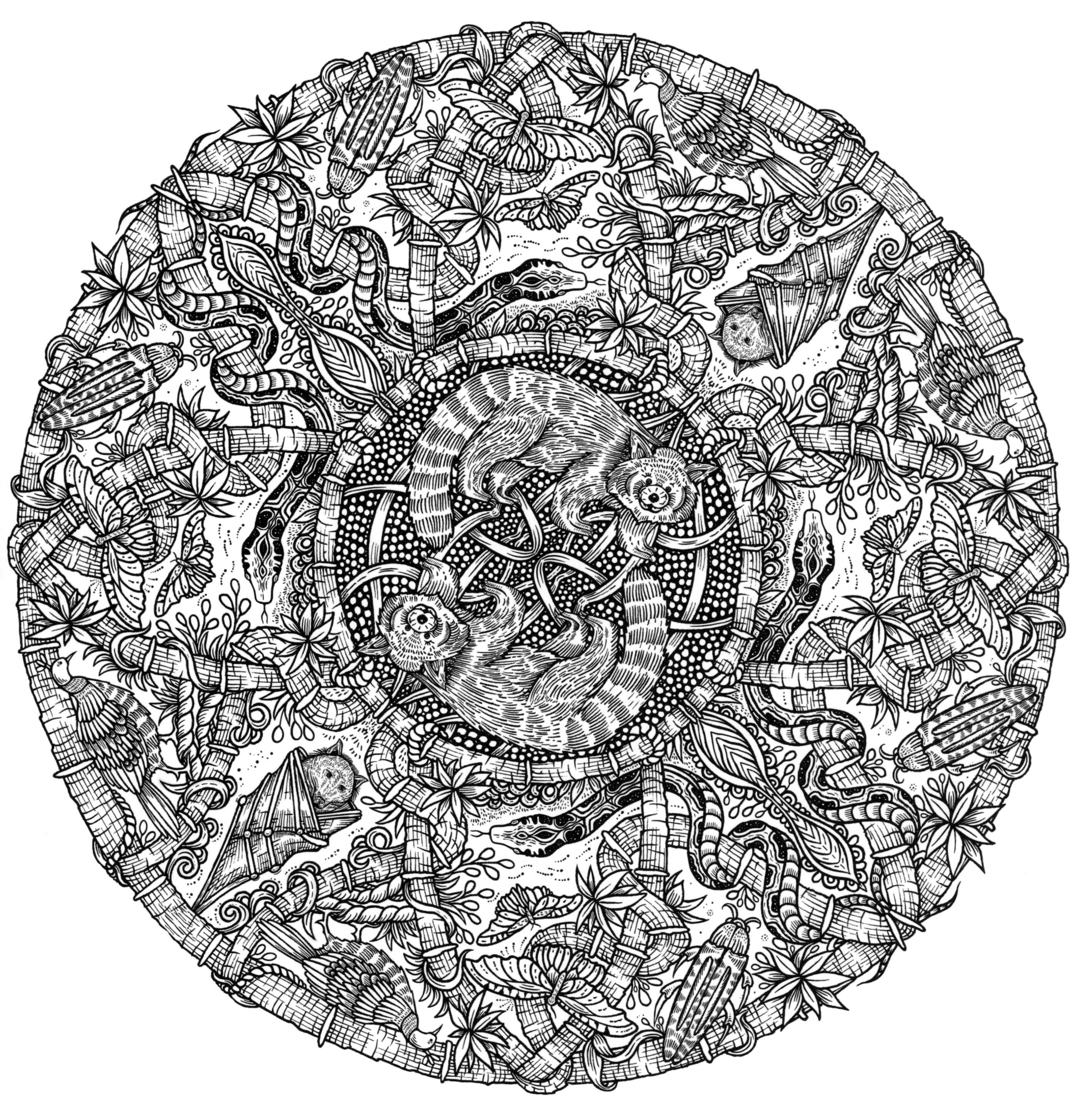

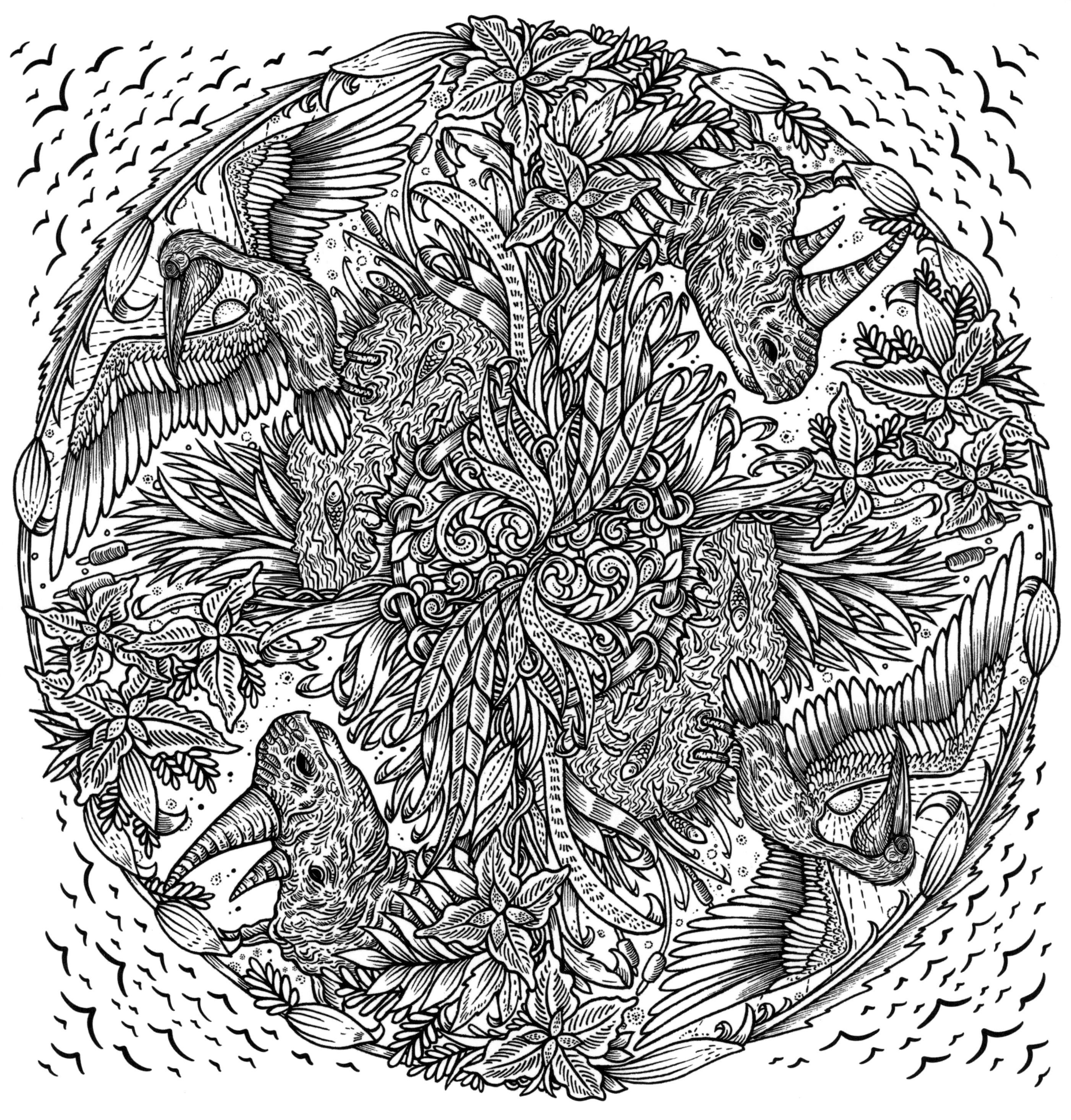

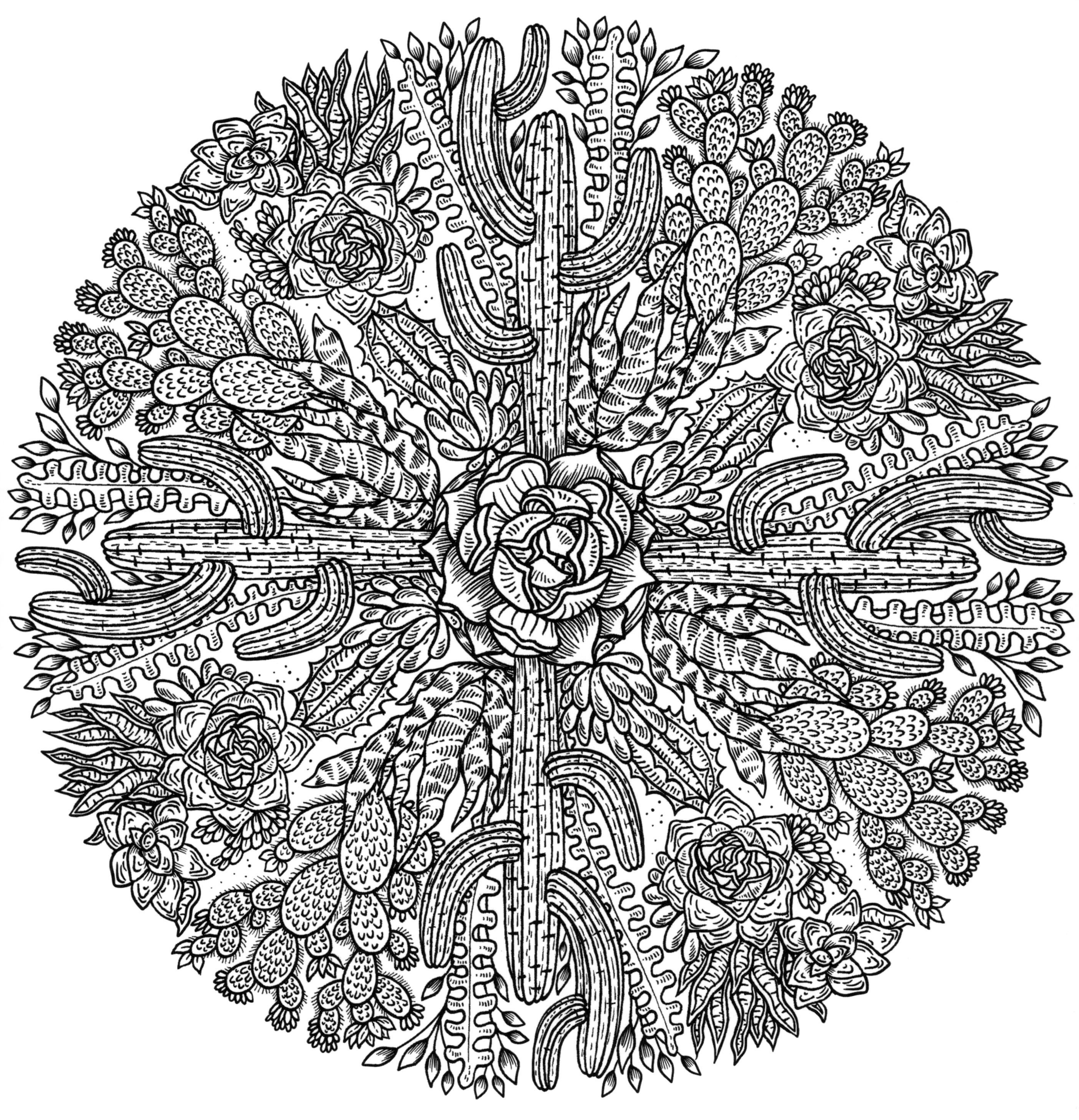

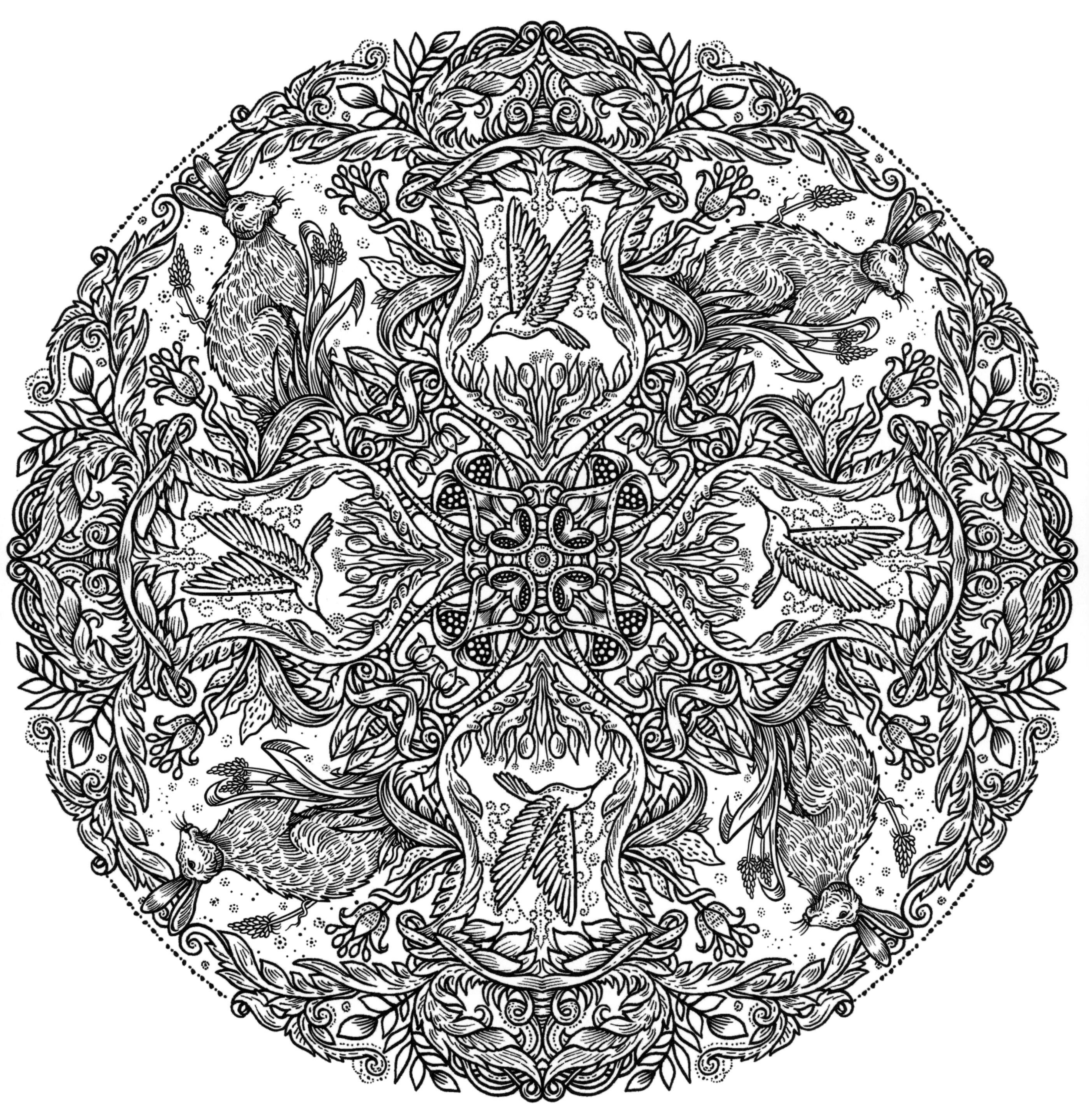

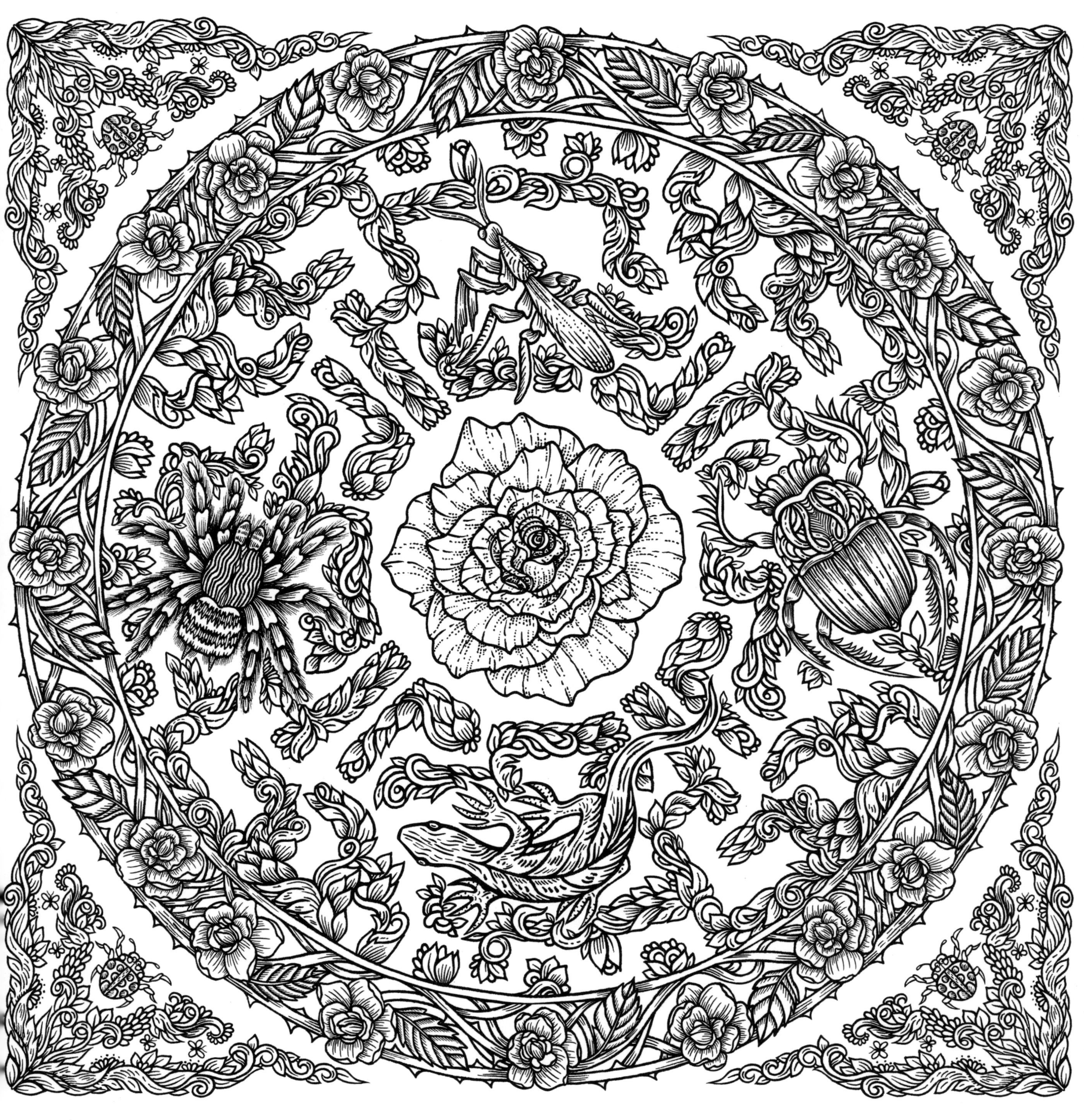

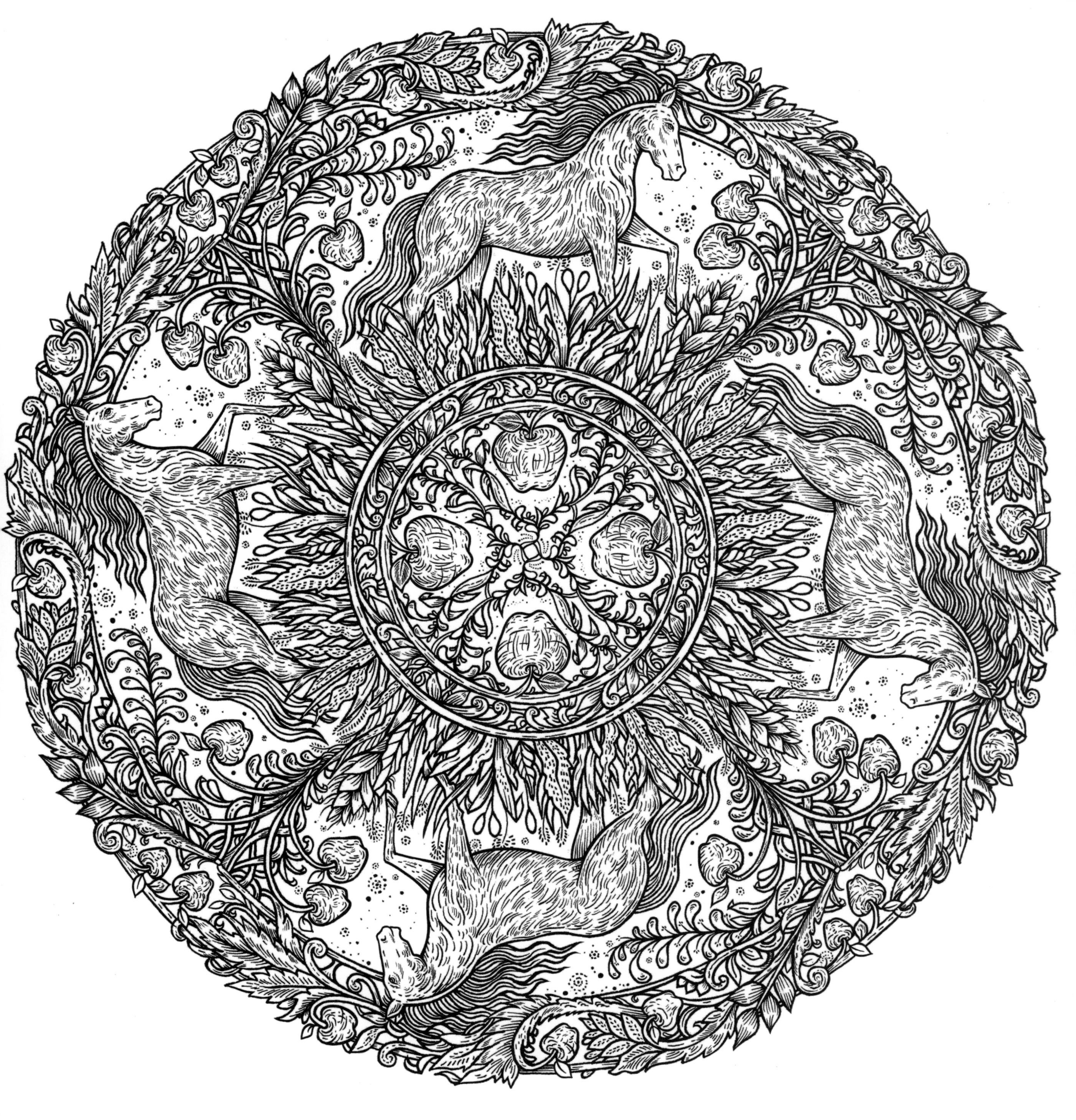

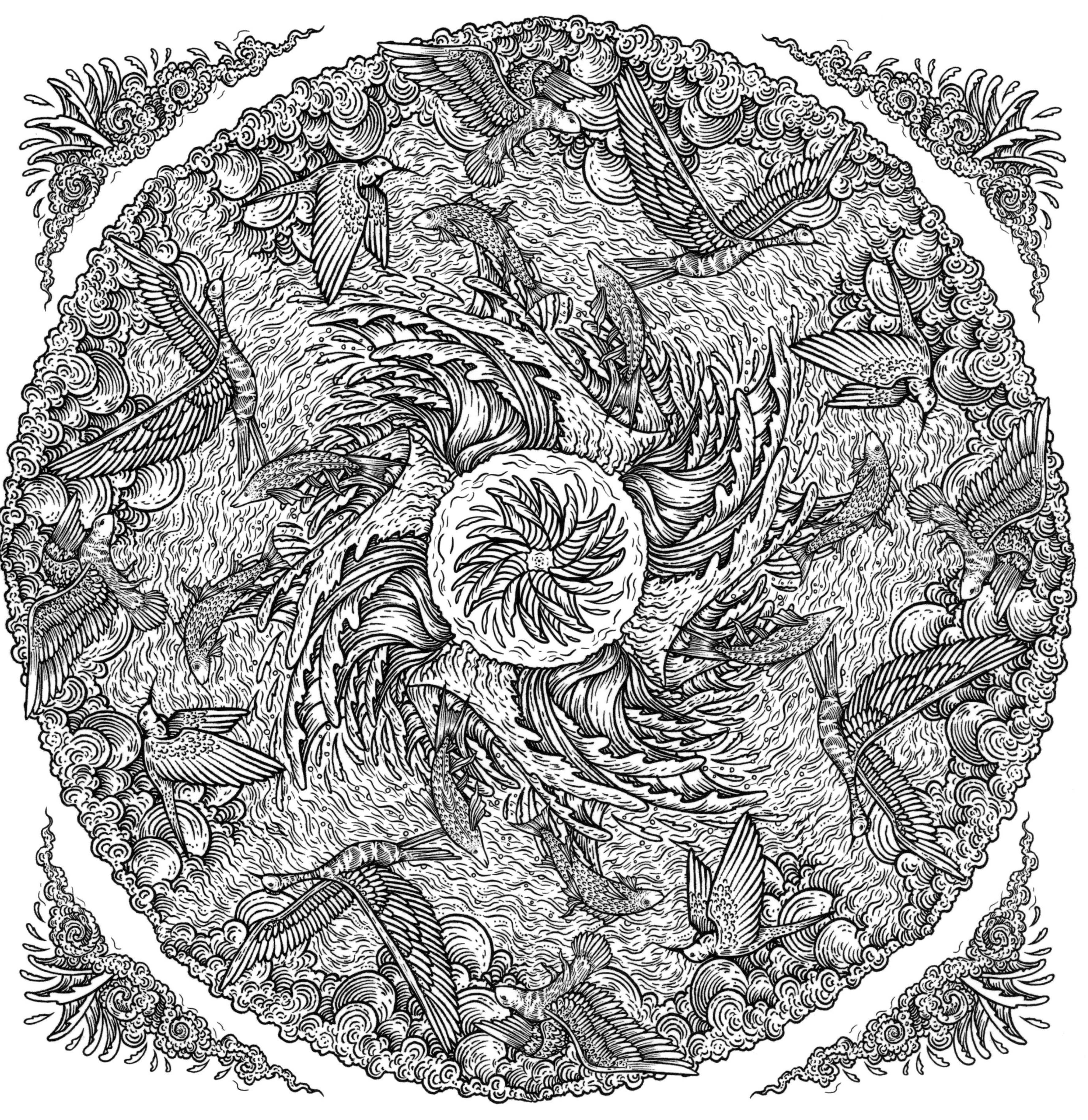

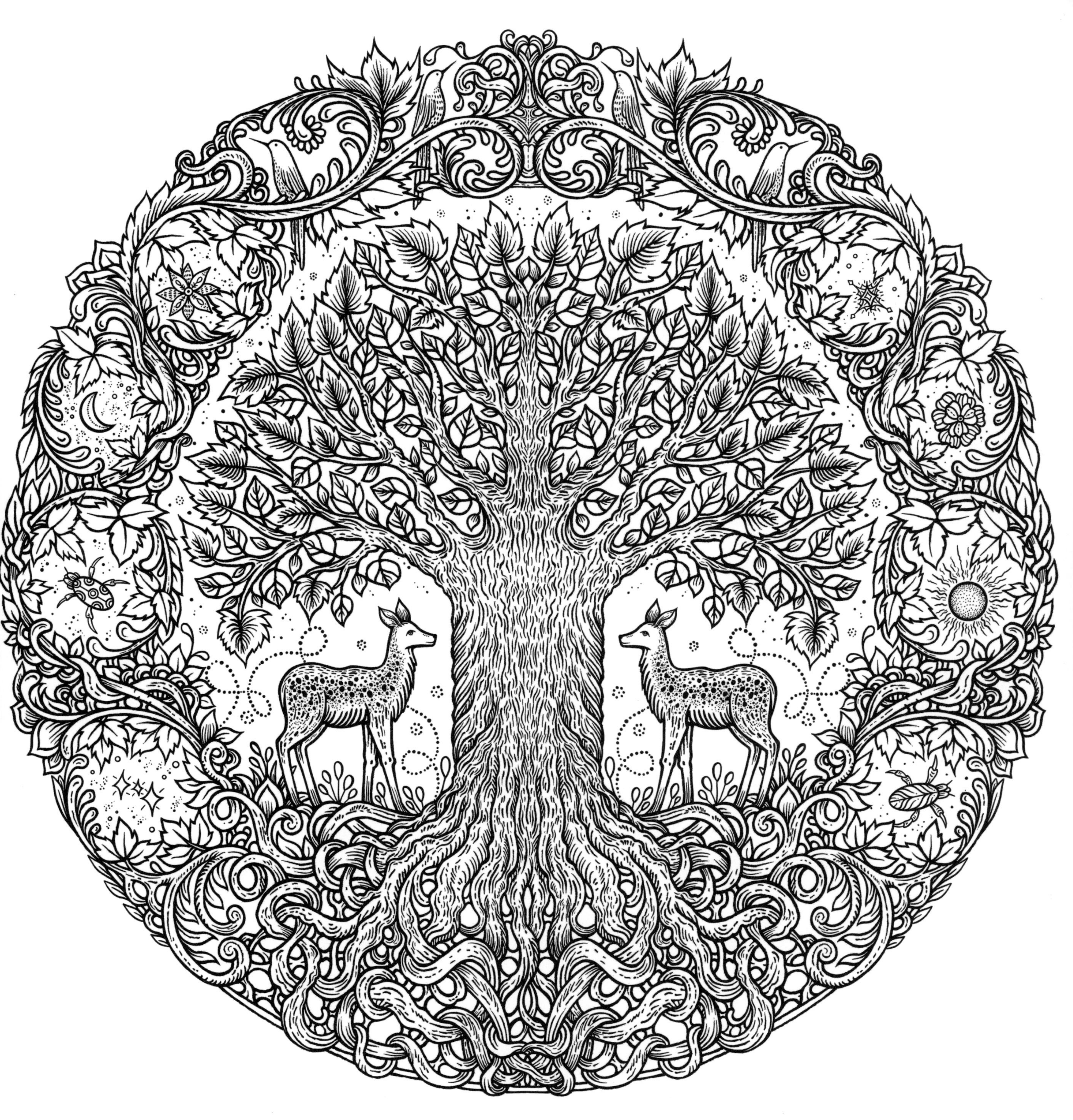

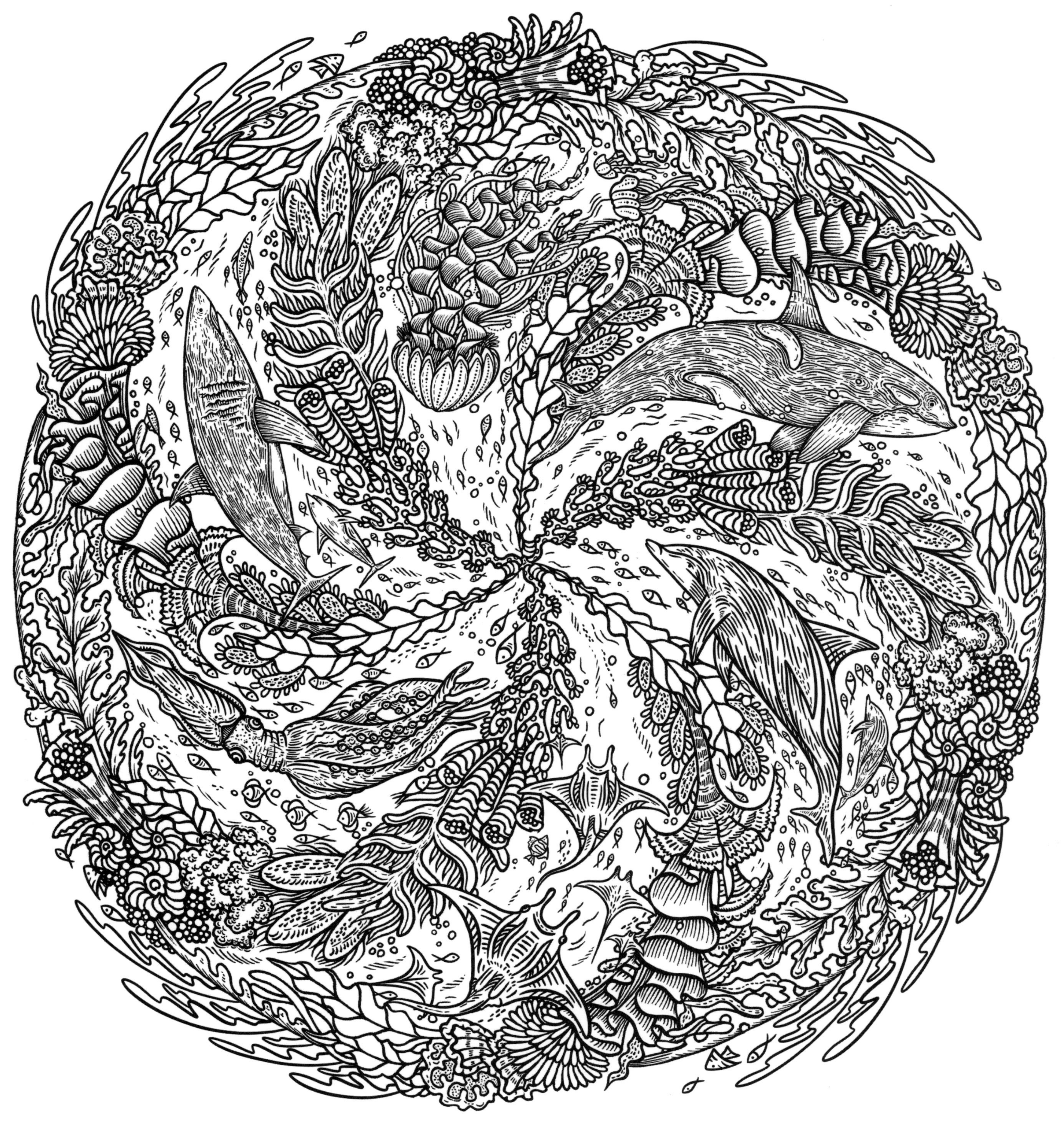

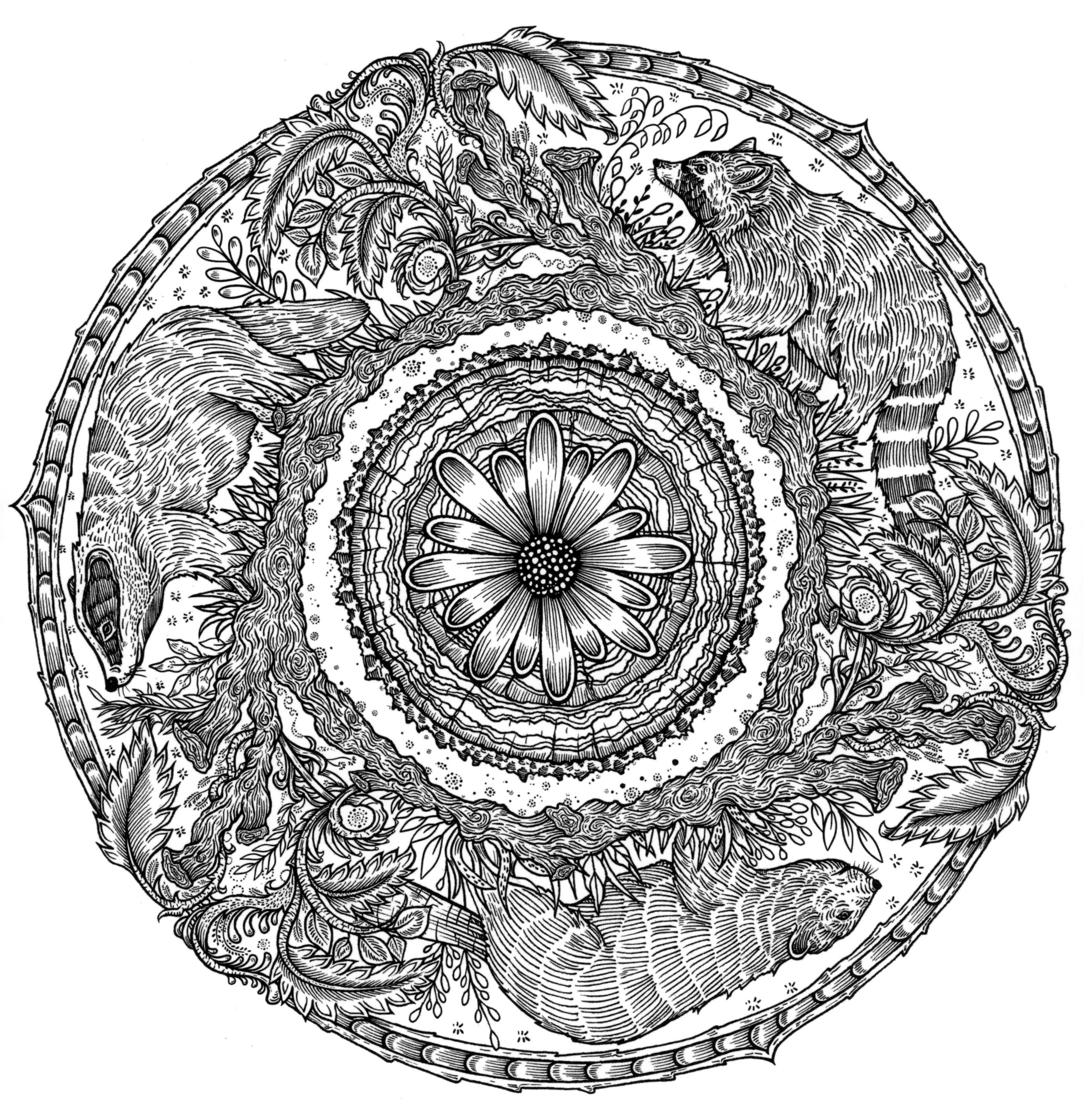

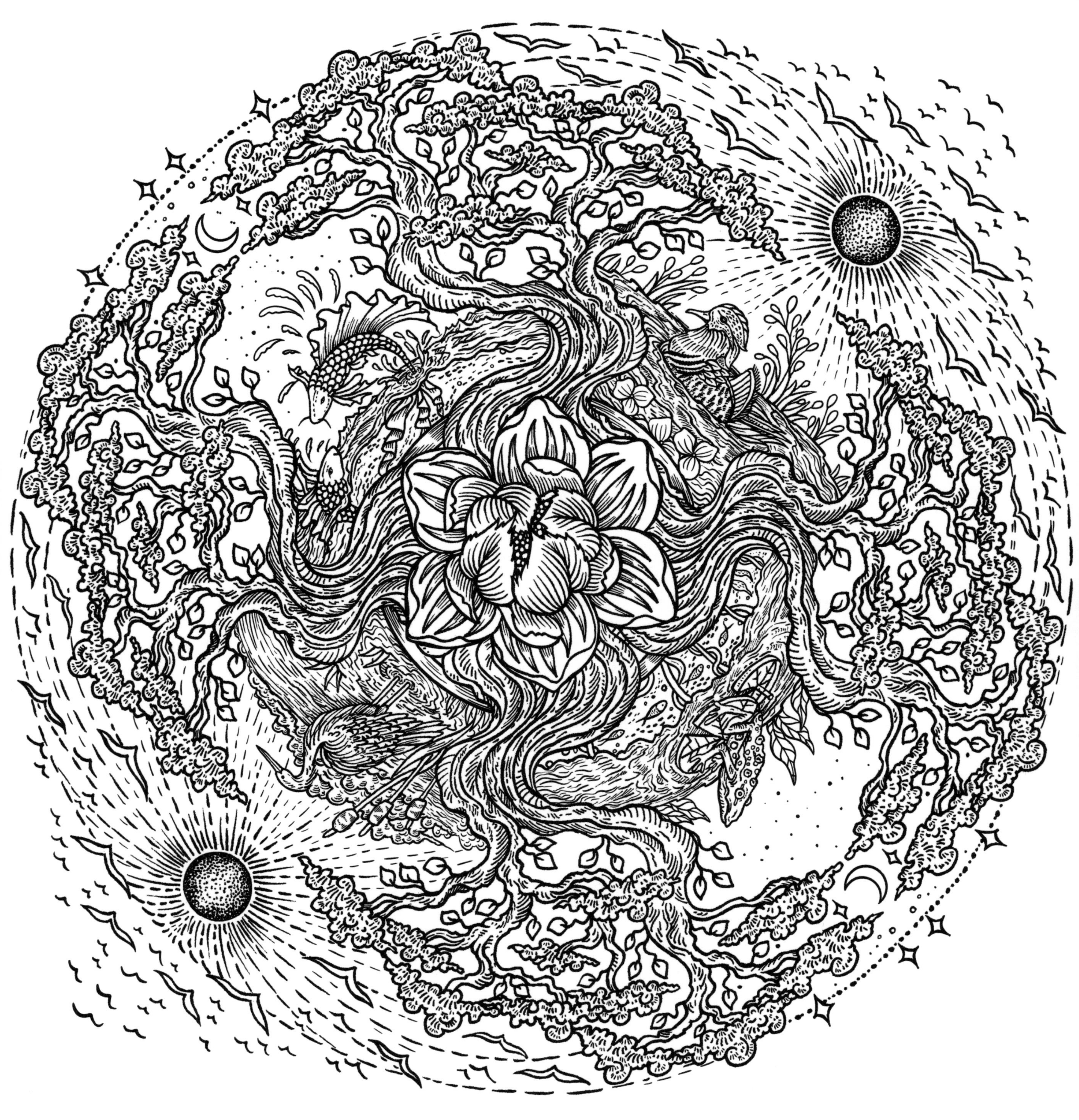

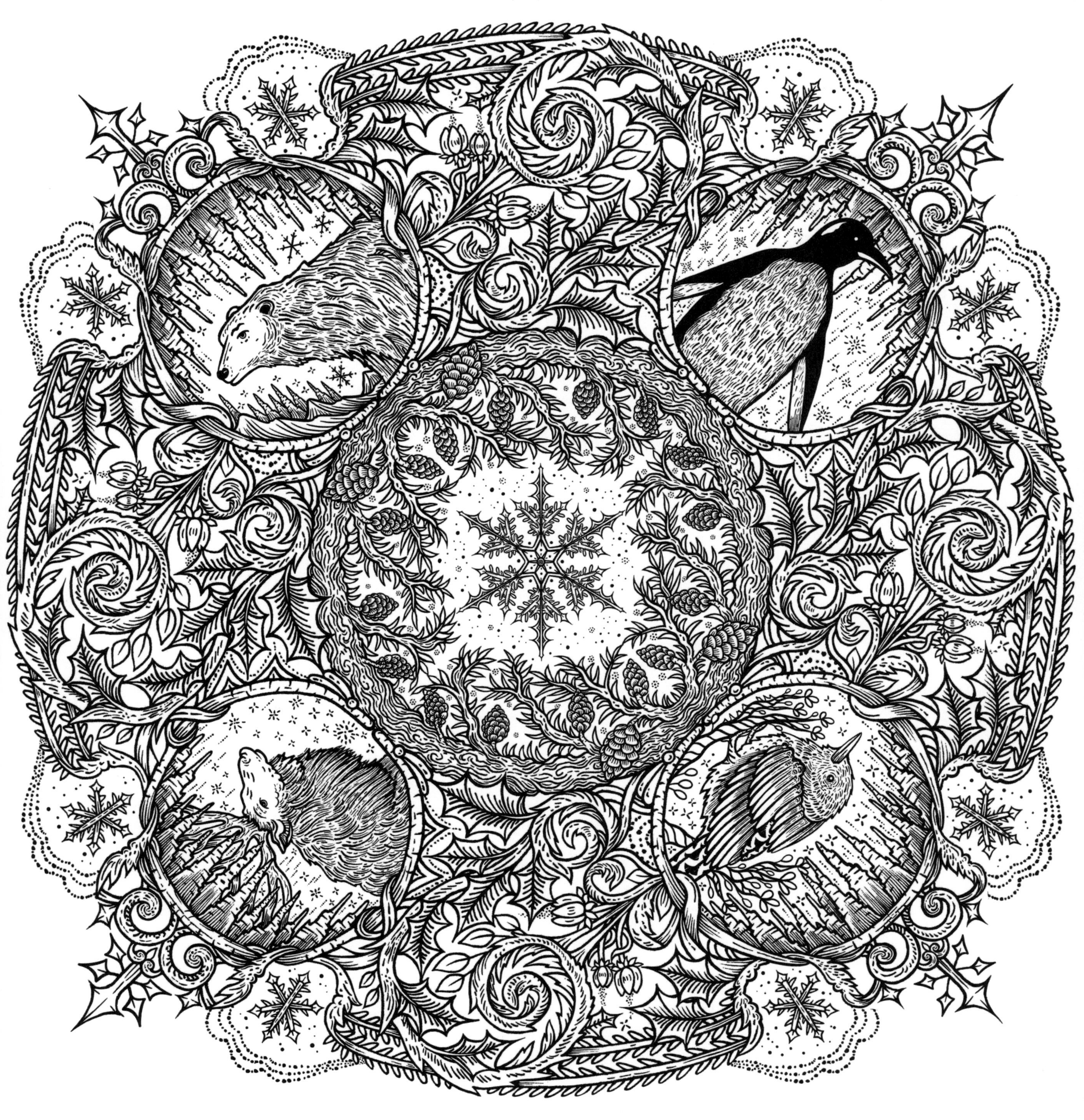

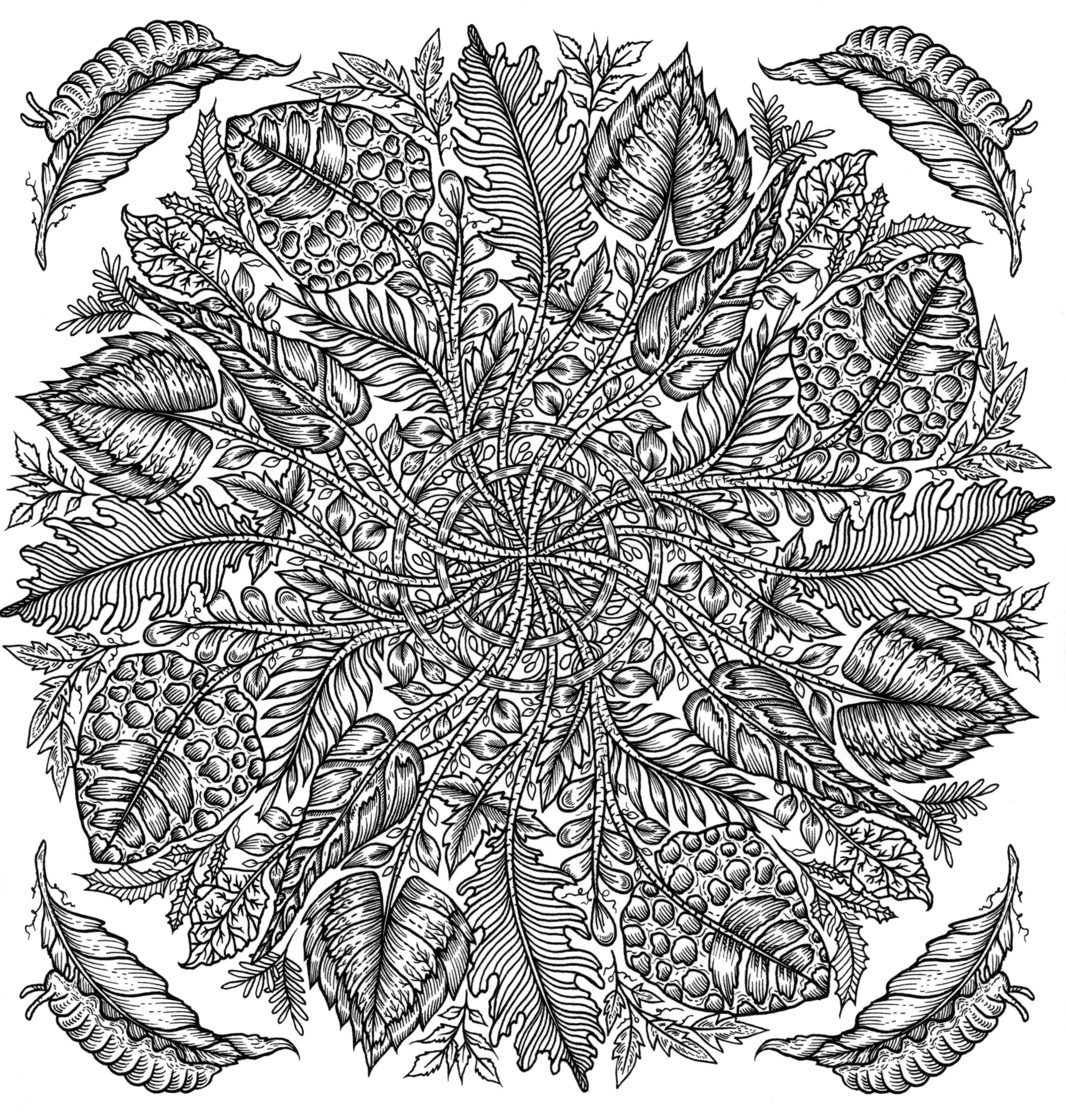

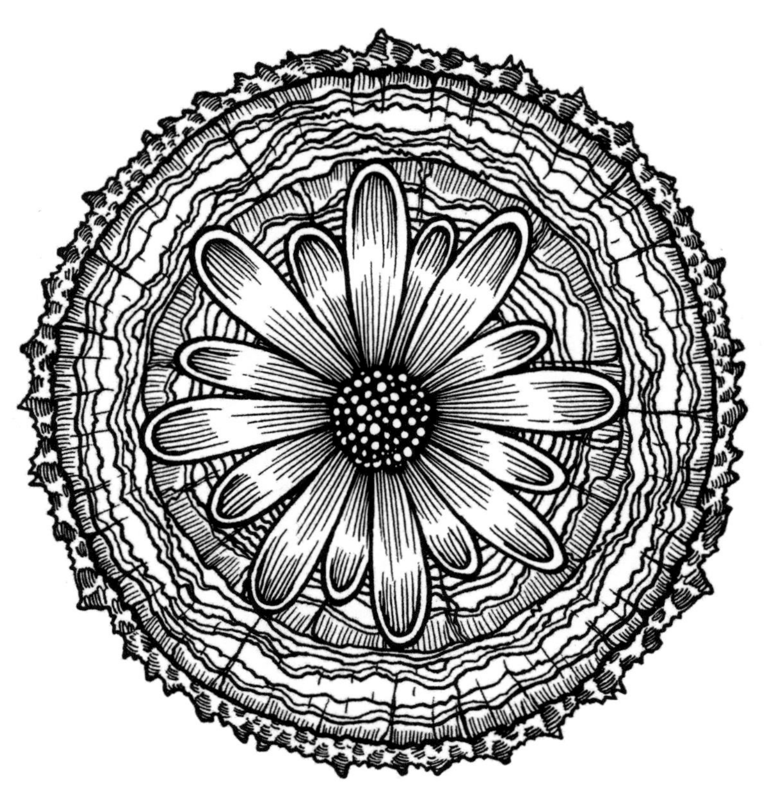